CW00556963

Unknowing God

Unknowing God

Toward a Post-Abusive Theology

Nicholas Peter Harvey
AND Linda Woodhead

CASCADE *Books* · Eugene, Oregon

UNKNOWING GOD
Toward a Post-Abusive Theology

Copyright © 2022 Wipf and Stock. All rights reserved. Except for brief quotations in critical publications or reviews, no part of this book may be reproduced in any manner without prior written permission from the publisher. Write: Permissions, Wipf and Stock Publishers, 199 W. 8th Ave., Suite 3, Eugene, OR 97401.

Cascade Books
An Imprint of Wipf and Stock Publishers
199 W. 8th Ave., Suite 3
Eugene, OR 97401

www.wipfandstock.com

PAPERBACK ISBN: 978-1-6667-1033-5
HARDCOVER ISBN: 978-1-6667-1034-2
EBOOK ISBN: 978-1-6667-1035-9

Cataloguing-in-Publication data:

Names: Harvey, Nicholas Peter, author. | Woodhead, Linda, author.

Title: Unknowing God : toward a post-abusive theology / by Nicholas Peter Harvey and Linda Woodhead.

Description: Eugene, OR: Cascade Books, 2022 | Includes bibliographical references and index.

Identifiers: ISBN 978-1-6667-1033-5 (paperback) | ISBN 978-1-6667-1034-2 (hardcover) | ISBN 978-1-6667-1035-9 (ebook)

Subjects: LCSH: Child sexual abuse by clergy. | Psychic trauma—Religious aspects—Christianity. | Dogma, Development of.

Classification: BV4910.45 U36 2022 (print) | BV4910 (ebook)

05/09/22

All Bible quotations are taken from the Revised Standard Version, copyright © 1946, 1952, and 1971 the Division of Christian Education of the National Council of the Churches of Christ in the United States of America.

"Oh Christianity, Christianity" by Stevie Smith, from COLLECTED POEMS OF STEVIE SMITH, copyright ©1972 by Stevie Smith. Reprinted by permission of New Directions Publishing Corp.

For John Stokes, our editor extraordinary.

A priest, philosopher, and prison chaplain whose gift is helping people see what they are trying to say.

CONTENTS

INTRODUCTION

THIS IS A BOOK born out of our experience of how bad ideas about God can destroy creative faith. We have had to fight against false ideas of "orthodoxy" put forward by our churches in order to find the divine in life. Although everyone will find their own way, we hope that it will be helpful to read about our engagements with the Christian past and other sources as we try to make sense of things.

We spent our early lives trying to become insiders in our respective churches, Catholic and Anglican, but it never quite worked. We were both trained in theology and taught candidates for the priesthood, but we felt unable to accept unreservedly the versions of Christianity that our churches supplied. Peter left the Benedictine monastery of Downside Abbey without any purchase on what his future might hold. He eventually became a tutor at Queen's ecumenical college and then a freelance writer. Linda began her career teaching doctrine and ethics at a Church of England theological college. She left to become an academic specializing in the study of religion and society.

We originally met at theological conferences, but our interest has always been more than merely professional. We maintained a friendship over the years by sending one another occasional reflections. We wrote in the midst of life, in order to understand. Our experiences with other faiths and none gradually gave us better insight into our own. This book grows out of a selection of these essays, which have been revised, revisited, and reordered. They offer sketches of the same landscape, shaped through mutual influence and criss-crossed in different directions.

We do not look away from abusive tendencies in religion. The language, imagery, and teachings of Christianity are not as unequivocally benign as some like to think. We have had to take a hard look at some unpleasant aspects of our churches, including thought control and the sexual abuse scandal; consider how theology is implicated; and face our own complicity.

The medieval mystical text *The Cloud of Unknowing* teaches that you can only experience God by forgetting and unknowing what you are most certain about. This cloud is something you have to pass through, not something you choose to enter. It is surprisingly hard to let go of a lurking childhood image of God, easier to rail against God in the manner of Richard Dawkins. But in letting go of God as an all-knowing, all-controlling being—and the privileges of being a deputy of omniscience—we have found something more compelling. When we have been able to let go of fearful, controlling anxiety, Spirit and spirits have often surprised us.

The views offered here do not fit any existing school. Whatever their faults, the kinds of Christianity in which we were raised—Tridentine Catholicism for Peter and rural Anglicanism for Linda—connect us to living traditions of Christian belief and practice that cannot be contained in any confessional formulae. Although we have had to abandon many of our starting assumptions, this is nothing like simple rejection. Leonard Cohen sings:

> Ring the bells that still can ring
> Forget your perfect offering
> There's a crack, a crack in everything
> That's how the light gets through.[1]

Faith, in our understanding, has nothing to do with passive reception of a set of propositions and rules: it is trust in awareness. "Watch!" says Jesus. You never know where and when the divine may break through or, more accurately, break out.

1. Leonard Cohen, "Anthem."

1. REWILDING GOD

LW

EARLY IN THE COURSE of a career spent studying religion, I asked the vicar of a local church whether he would mind if I interviewed some members of the congregation. "That's OK," he said, "but please don't ask them what they believe because it upsets them." In talking to Christians then and since, I have been struck by how reluctant many are to talk about belief. There is a worry that they might say the wrong thing.

This anxiety was high among students I helped train for ordination in the Church of England. They did not want to make a mistake for fear of being labeled ignorant or unorthodox. Anxiety hovered over our discussions of God like a suffocating cloud. In many congregations, I have encountered something similar: either the offering up of doctrinal formulas in place of a heartfelt answer, or the suggestion that I should talk to someone more competent, often a husband or pastor "who knows more than me." The urge to match up to the proper standards of belief is of a piece with a desire to tidy up all aspects of life. We think that if we iron things out they will become clearer, more rational, easier to control.

Religious leaders are enthusiasts for intellectual tidying. Christianity has more creeds, confessions, catechisms, and doctrinal treatises than any other religion. Often, they have a political as well as a theological purpose. In the Church of England today, ordinands still have to swear allegiance to God and the monarch while bishops promise to "banish and drive away all erroneous and strange doctrines contrary to God's Word."[1] When, early in the history of the churches, Eusebius depicted the Christian God as a mighty sovereign directing human affairs, his not-so-hidden agenda was the integration of church and empire under the Roman Emperor Constantine,

---

1. Church of England, "Oath of Allegiance" and "Consecration of Bishops."

1

his patron.[2] Loyalty to God and loyalty to group get mixed up, conformity to a standard of orthodoxy becoming the test of both.

Christian images of God have softened in recent generations. Gentler family values and more egalitarian attitudes have made the idea of a heavenly Judge who consigns sinners to hell unpalatable. Feminists have questioned the maleness of God and charismatic evangelicals have promoted a God who has a more cozy and approachable majesty. What has not changed is the idea that God favors churches with a big "C" (like the Catholic Church) and a small "c" (congregations and their buildings). When marriage laws were reformed in England and Wales in 1994, for example, church leaders insisted that marriage could only take place in a church building. They assumed that God could not be relied upon to show up in the wild.

It is not only Christians who like to tame and tidy things up. So do supposedly more tolerant kinds of New Age spirituality that proclaim that there is a mystical oneness at the heart of things that unites all faiths and believers. What is forgotten is that calling God "One" is as much a metaphor as talking about God's "right hand." The messy reality of human beings' manifold encounters with deities and other spiritual beings is brushed aside for a higher truth that "we"—the insiders—know about. A God within can operate very much like a God up above.

An extreme attempt at tidying up the divine is found in the philosophy of religion. Much energy has been expended in arriving at an agreed definition of God. The result is peculiar: a being who is singular (monotheist, universal, sufficient); personal but spiritual (not embodied); and overwhelming (omnipotent, omniscient, and omni-benevolent).[3] What is being offered is an omni-God: the all-powerful, all-knowing, all-good God who is taught in philosophy, debated on TV, and ridiculed by nonbelievers. This is also the God of late-night arguments after a few drinks. It is the God that atheists do not believe in.

The omni-God generates many intractable puzzles, including the so-called "problem of evil." "Is [God] willing to prevent evil, but not able?" asked the skeptic in philosopher David Hume's *Dialogues*. "Then is he impotent. Is he able, but not willing? then is he malevolent. Is he both able

2. Barnes, *Constantine and Eusebius*.

3. Yujin Nagasawa speaks of an "omni God," though his contribution is to defend a "maximal God" characterized by the maximal consistent set of knowledge, power, and benevolence. See Nagasawa, *Maximal God*.

and willing? whence then is evil?"[4] Here the problem of evil is the problem of how to reconcile an all-good, all-powerful God with a world of suffering. There is no satisfactory answer. Two world wars, the holocaust, and the atrocities of totalitarianism have only sharpened the problem. But take away this omni-monotheism, and the problem looks very different.

When I was a student of theology, Petru Dumitriu's *To The Unknown God* was all the rage. Writing in the context of communist oppression in Romania, Dumitriu recounted his struggle with doubts that constantly threatened to overwhelm his faith in God. His descriptions of atrocities and corruptions are more compelling than his descriptions of flimsy and fleeting encounters with divine grace. As he struggles to hold on to faith, the most he can affirm is the importance of remaining open to the question of God. Prayer is merely waiting in hope: "If God so wishes it: grace comes, or it does not come. If it does not come, all this will fall into dust, a little handful of ash falling in the void. But I am waiting."[5]

Dumitriu's non-conclusive conclusion about God's existence is similar to Simone Weil's in *Waiting on God,* or Samuel Becket's in *Waiting for Godot.* Like Dumitriu, they cannot reconcile the existence of God with the horrific reality of suffering and abandonment. The best that Weil can do is to speculate that the deity must choose, out of love, not to exercise omnipotence. This idea of a voluntary withdrawal of divine power seems like allowing the omni-God to have his cake and eat it too. It is as unsatisfactory as the idea of a "servant leader" applied to a church dignitary.

When I read *To the Unknown God* today, I find myself wondering why I took it so seriously. Years of studying religiosity around the world must have changed me. Even in monotheistic cultures, I have found that the sort of omni-God that Weil and Dumitriu have in mind is the exception, not the rule. In India, China, and Japan that is even more obvious. A visit to a Kali temple or ancestral shrine makes the point. Dumitriu agonized over how the omni-God could allow terrible things to happen, but never once thought to question his understanding of the divine. We get trapped by failures of the theological imagination, tied up in definitions and orthodoxies, anxious about falling out of line or looking stupid. Some ideas of God are promoted as orthodox and acceptable, others are laughed at and dismissed.

4. Hume, *Dialogues Concerning Natural Religion*, 106.

5. Dumitriu, *To the Unknown God*, 150.

To maintain "orthodoxy" calls for a censorship of experience. I am haunted by the memory of a young Christian woman I met in a megachurch in the USA who was suffering from an aggressive cancer. Her belief in an all-powerful, all-good, all-loving God meant that she could only blame herself for what was happening. If only she could have more faith, she would be healed; if only she could trust Jesus fully, she would be less fearful. It was painful to witness her struggle to remain cheerful and optimistic. To hold on to God meant denying anger, pain, and despair. The anthropologist Anna Strhan notes how much time conservative Christian groups devote to banishing doubts and reconstructing coherence.[6] Faith may be a way of denying the complexities and ambiguities of our lives.

No wonder many people experience an all-loving, all-good God as fearsomely oppressive. He is a constant reminder of human deficiency. Worship at the throne of this being can seem like an endless, humiliating round of saying "sorry" and "thank you." Visiting a Church of England primary school recently, I saw on the wall prayers that the children had written and illustrated. Each and every one was a variation on the theme of: "Dear God. Thank you for the world all around us. It is very kind of you to give it to us." It reminded me of the good manners that my parents tried to instill in me as a child, extended to God above. With such a God, though, it is never enough.

I cannot remember now whether I began to have intimations of a different kind of divinity before I gave up on the omni-God, or whether it was giving up on the omni-God that opened me to new experiences of the divine. The arguments against an all-powerful, all-good deity played a part, but there was a deeper transformation as well. I know that a year spent abroad was a turning point. I found myself drawn back time and again to a particular oak tree in a forest, majestic and ancient, known to locals as "Grandmother." Standing a respectful distance away, I felt a wise presence that communicated with me in different ways on different occasions: through sounds, glimpsed sights, a feeling, or an inner sense. Many times when I visited, I felt myself connected to a powerful force that blended with me but was separate and greater than me. It was the tree, but it was much more than the tree—just as the bread of the Eucharist is the bread, but much more than the bread. It was a "real presence." The theologian Mark Wallace points out that the Holy Spirit appears at Jesus' baptism as a pigeon, and that it is only our squeamishness that makes us

6. Strhan, *Aliens and Strangers*.

use the word *dove* and doubt that God can really be a bird as well as more than a bird, just as God can really be bread.[7]

My awareness was growing and leading me to new places. Some were in the past, in the sense that I was able to reconnect with buried memories: as a child finding peace in a grove of hawthorn trees by a stream; gathered up in joy in a church service at midnight; touched unexpectedly by the presence of the dead; visited in dreams.

Today, the line between the human and the divine, the natural and the spiritual, no longer seems so sharp. My toleration for different ways of imagining God/s and Spirit/s is much greater. I have been freed from the compulsion to find a single narrative thread in the Bible, to set Christianity apart from other sources of inspiration, or to tame and tidy up the ways in which God appears to me and others.

"God of Abraham, God of Isaac, God of Jacob—not of the philosophers and scholars," said Pascal of his epiphany. The God of philosophers, scholars, and preachers is often imposed on the Bible and on us with such insistence that we see but do not see the more interesting picture of a multiplicity of divine and semi-divine beings, of gods, goddesses, angels, and demons. There is an entire dictionary devoted to the deities and demons in the Bible.[8] One of the names for God in the Hebrew scriptures is "Elohim," which is plural not singular: gods not God. There are goddesses as well as gods.[9] Even in texts where there is a supreme God, this deity struggles against rival deities, seldom alone. The "Lord God of hosts" is a ruler of angelic armies. "God has taken his place in the divine council; in the midst of the gods he holds judgment," says Psalm 82:1.

Christian belief in the Trinity and the incarnation of God in Jesus Christ is impossible to reconcile with strict monotheism, as Muslim friends remind me. When Jesus speaks of his own divine status, he uses texts from the Jewish Scriptures. In Acts when Paul preaches to the Athenians, he doesn't deny the existence of their deities. His argument sounds distinctly pantheist: "'in him [God] we live and move and have our being.' As even some of your [Greek] poets have said, 'For we are indeed his offspring'" (Acts 17:28). Even when later Christian evangelists condemned other people's gods, they did not deny their reality but categorized them as lesser beings or demons. The deeply Christian culture of medieval Ireland is characterized by a historian

7. Wallace, *When God Was a Bird*.

8. van der Toorn et al., eds., *Dictionary of Deities and Demons in the Bible*.

9. Becking et al., eds., *Only One God?*

as "monotheistic to a certain extent."[10] The Reformation was an attempt to do some heavenly cleansing. Protestants believed that the Catholic faith—with Mary, the saints, angels, sacraments, holy wells, and shrines—needed to be drastically, violently tidied up. But no amount of cleansing can turn Christianity's rich tradition of belief and practice into a single orthodoxy with an omni-benevolent God at its heart.

The Bible speaks of God/s as darkness, cloud, fire, a hammer, an abyss.[11] These Gods are at various times murderous, irascible, unreasonable, unfair, wild, and cruel. They are manifest as fire, thunder, and wind. Far from just praising and thanking them, people wrestle with them, argue with them (and sometimes win), are crushed by them. The divine can be as tender as a mother, as passionate as a lover, as impersonal as a judge, as cruel as fate: "He snatches away; who can hinder him? Who will say to him, 'What doest thou?'" (Job 9:12). Jesus says that God makes his rain to fall on the just and unjust, and that the tower of Siloam crushed those it fell on irrespective of what they deserved. "Does evil befall a city, unless the Lord has done it?" asks the prophet Amos (3:6). God/s are not bound by conventional morals.

There is no doubting the fact that the divine appears differently to different people, even in the same situation. If I manage to make people feel safe enough to speak candidly, even in dogmatic religious groups, I am amazed how much variation there is in personal belief. To some, God is an impersonal force, to others personal, to some an energy, to others a being. Some people experience many gods and spirits, some only one. Some believe there are spiritual entities who dwell not just in heavenly realms above, but in subterranean ones below, as well as those who dwell in "middle earth" alongside us—like fairy people and spirits of places—not to mention those beings like angels who move between worlds. You never know until you ask, and we are all guilty of making assumptions.

The American anthropologist Jill Dubisch recounts an experience during a research trip to Stonehenge when, in the midst of that ring of massive stones, she felt something "deep, dark, and strong" come over her:

> A very powerful presence, a sense of a deep primal energy coming
> from beneath the stone circle, a power which was beyond words,
> which made what was happening in our ritual seem like mere fluff

---

10. Borsje, "Monotheistic to a Certain Extent."

11. A darkness (Exodus 20:21), a cloud (Exodus 13:21), a fire (Exodus 3:2), a hammer (Jeremiah 23:29), an abyss (Habbakuk 3:10)—amongst other examples.

on the surface of things, a power both underlying and transcending the rituals we humans devised, a power—and here is the crucial point—neither male nor female, but instead beyond gender.[12]

Dubisch's immediate thought is: "I've come home." When celebrations for Stanley Kubrick's film *2001: A Space Odyssey* took place in the real 2001, its original fans turned out not to be film critics but teenage boys. In their retrospective appreciations they said there was a lot of it they did not understand at the time, but it opened their minds to infinity and amazing possibilities—to space in the broadest sense.

The God that many of us were taught about as children was too restrictive. As we grew older we looked for a bigger, more truthful, reality—whether secular or religious. If "God" becomes a dead letter, or a deadening one, we are better off without God. Loosening up my neurotic monotheism, I found the divine in new ways—without necessarily being able to give a coherent account. It does not all have to add up.

12. Dubisch, "Religion Without Gender?," 35.

2. STATES OF MIND AND ALLEGIANCE TO CREEDS

NPH

YEARS AGO I BECAME a disciple of someone who died suddenly, in extreme pain of mind and body. He did so in the midst of profound conflict in the religious community of which we were at the time both members. Most people saw what happened as either a tragedy or a cautionary tale, or both. For me it was part of a revelatory process, in the light of which I looked at the evangelists' accounts of the death and resurrection of Jesus with amazed recognition. It came to seem obvious that the only context in which belief in the resurrection of Jesus made sense was that of a traumatic bereavement.

It could be argued that I was in danger of anachronistic projection onto the first Christians of modern experiences of bereavement. At least as problematic was my uncritical support for the claim emerging from his disciples' bereavement that Jesus was the savior of the world. Is this not to support a claim which excludes too much? In those days I was able to brush aside these objections.

My discipleship of this man in his life, his death, and its aftermath, enabled me to sustain a version of the Christian story that retained key elements from the religion of my childhood. The implicit suggestion of that religion was that all those of good will, whether of other faiths or none, would in the end see things our way—the Catholic way. No satisfactory account was given of why so very few showed the slightest sign of doing so. What was never in doubt was the credibility of our Roman Catholic credal system, its absolute and obvious superiority, intellectually and spiritually, to anything else on offer. The contemporary church has to some extent adjusted to the cultural pluralism characteristic of our world, so that my childhood religion already looks antediluvian. But the claim to a distinctive certainty in faith, and specifically in the content of faith, persists. It is this which not only remained unquestioned, but was given a new lease of life, by my post-traumatic state. I have moved on since then.

My present conviction is that we know too much about other religious and philosophical claims to hold to the uniqueness of Jesus in that all-inclusive or all-surpassing sense. The outright assertion that the risen Jesus is the savior of the world wipes out so much that comes from other sources of wisdom, well-being, and inspiration. The old apologetic presented the ancient Greek philosophers as part of a providential preparation of humanity for the coming of Jesus. But Islam came after Christianity, took the Greeks with at least equal seriousness, and reached different conclusions about Jesus. First-century Judaism, like Christianity, is a product of earlier Jewish religion. Each saw itself as the authentic development of that tradition, but disagreed, as they continue to do, about Jesus. These examples could be multiplied.

In my post-traumatic reading of the New Testament what was calling the shots was not any text but my present experience. I had once supposed that my master alone had a definitive wisdom. This controlling assumption took root when the monastic community to which he and I belonged was all the world to me. So it must have been, I reasoned, for the disciples of Jesus. But the underlying conviction was produced and sustained by current events. Interest in the story of Jesus was a kind of extrapolation from or commentary on what I saw to be happening amongst us.

Recognition of this does not invalidate my then reading of the texts, but it changes the status, and therefore the consequences, of that reading. My insistence on a particular form of traumatic bereavement as the indispensable setting for resurrection-faith is relativized. It becomes one among many versions of stories that have in the course of their history been the occasion of a great diversity of interpretations. It is no more possible to say outright "This is what these stories mean" than it is to say "This is what Shakespeare's *King Lear* means." Catholic tradition has tried to get beyond this by stressing the role of the church as the authoritative interpreter, with the implication that Catholic teaching, unlike Shakespearean criticism, is specially protected from error. But this claim gets us no further in the face of the range of meanings sanctioned or at least taken seriously by the church at one time or other.

What requires further comment is the fact that my resistance to the idea of projection, and my christological exclusiveness, were untouched by intellectual arguments that now seem cogent. What is at issue here is not arguments but states of mind. Reflecting in retrospect on the exalted frame of mind in which he had found himself at the time of his young wife's death, P. J. Kavanagh writes in *The Perfect Stranger*: "The sky would not have held all the things I could believe."[1] I never believed that my master was the savior of the world. But I saw him as the savior of my world, and perhaps the difference is minimal. He was the person whose insight cut as deep as it is possible to cut, and who could be relied upon to have insight: whose death, therefore, had to be of absolute significance, though thenceforth he was available only through memory. In my bereavement I believed all manner of things about the significance of our community, which later experience called into question. It also called into question my totalizing tendency toward the traditions about Jesus. What had powered the story for me could no longer do so in any straightforward way, for the context in my life had gone.

All this is worth rehearsing in order to raise questions about belief: about why we believe what we believe, or how passionately held beliefs can come and go. If states of mind rather than arguments are the point, we need to ask what factors dispose us in the direction of particular states. Autobiography is inescapable here. It is not just a way of exemplifying or fleshing out a point which can be made in other ways: it is itself the point.

What disposed me in early adult life for the form of discipleship with which this chapter began? The person I then was took in and held to this man's ideas to an extent that no one else did, though many were influenced by him. Some people say they believe in the resurrection of Jesus because the inspired Scriptures tell of it, or because this belief is the abiding tradition of the church. But what is the predisposition to endow these sources with such authority that counter-arguments cannot be taken seriously? What are the present emotional realities that impel or sustain such allegiances?

Archbishop John Quinn notes among Catholics a reverence for the mystical role of the papacy, which creates "a deep psychological barrier to speaking in critical terms about policies, declarations or actions of the Pope."[2] Notice that the barrier is psychological rather than theological. It was manifested in Cardinal Cormac Murphy-O'Connor's response to an interviewer's questions about contraception, women priests, and other items in a checklist of questions addressed to leading Catholics. Agreeing

---

1. Kavanagh, *Perfect Stranger,* 180.
2. Kaiser, "Review of John R. Quinn."

with the pope of the day on each of these, Murphy-O'Connor said, "I am a man of the Church," as if there was no need for him to say any more. Again, arguments are not the point when emotional allegiances are in play. We need to go much further than John Quinn by asking what function this and comparable frames of mind are performing in the person and the group concerned. What form of identity is being preserved, or striven for, or denied by way of such allegiances? As my identity becomes looser the thinking changes.

3. TAKING RESPONSIBILITY
FOR GOD

LW

A CHILDHOOD FRIEND OF mine, taunted beyond endurance by her younger brother, retaliated by standing in the middle of the lawn, staring into the heavens and imploring: "God kill David!" It was a thrilling moment, and I assumed that her parents were right to be angry. Now I see there is something to be understood here, and mere moralism is not going to help.

Critics of religion often focus on the dangers posed by a dark and wrathful God who can be used to justify violence, without realizing that a God of light and love can be just as dangerous. If we believe that we have a clear channel to God, understood as the paragon of virtue and power, then there is a part of our life—the spiritual part—where normal standards don't apply. Here, in the secret garden of the alone with the Alone, I find ultimate validation. I am accountable to God, and God is accountable to no one.

It is an exercise in futility to try to have a conversation with someone who claims to be speaking for God. It's like arguing with an operative who says: "I'm just following the rules, I don't make them." When there is no sense of responsibility, fallibility—or humor—it is hard to make a human connection. Conflating theological conviction with God-given revelation results in an uncritical endorsement of whatever time-bound version of truth has captured our allegiance. Spiritual experience may be transformative, but what it cannot be is a "sky hook" that hoists me above human limitations.

There is a world of difference between saying that I am responsible to God and saying that I am responsible to the divine in you. Public inquiries into historical child abuse in religious institutions reveal how dangerous personal piety can be. In the Independent Inquiry into Child Sexual Abuse in England and Wales, an Anglican archdeacon reported that one of his clergy, who was later sentenced to ten years' imprisonment for thirty-six separate sex offences against sixteen different children, "took the view that he had been forgiven by God, his slate was therefore wiped clean . . . as if the abuse hadn't happened."[1] Here, forgiveness is interpreted as a kind of third-party transaction in which someone can confess their sins before God and be absolved without having to dirty their hands with the difficult business of trying to learn from and repair the damage done to another human being.

Religion is dangerous when it serves as a splitting wedge that separates off what we find most difficult to face up to and exiles it to a secret compartment. In an account of his conversion to Roman Catholicism, Sohrab Ahmari talks in exalted tones about the high mass in London's Brompton Oratory. He speaks of it as a holy place, set apart from the banality and corruption of human affairs.[2] Reviewing the book, the church historian Philip Jenkins senses unreality: "It's assuredly Catholic, indeed deeply eucharistic. But it is also idiosyncratic and idealized: the faith of someone who seems to have missed the past half century or so."[3] In his pious ecstasy, Ahmari has raised his eyes to heaven and averted them from church history and scandal. Although atheist critics often speak of religion as a "crutch," it operates here more like a hovercraft—a vehicle for skimming over the surface of things without getting one's feet wet. This magical levitation works best when belief in an original religious innocence can be maintained. Theological distinctions like that between a mystical and temporal church, or between a redeemed and an unredeemed sinner, make this possible. Pious protestations about everyone being sinful have served as a cover story for abuses and an excuse for not listening to complaints and accusations.

Even after the public inquiries, there is a reluctance in church circles to admit that theology and piety are often implicated in abuse. The Anglican Bishop of Guildford describes his beating by the serial abuser John Smyth as a "violent, excruciating and shocking" event, but goes on to say that, "absolutely nothing that happened in the Smyth shed was the natural fruit of any Christian theology that I've come across before or since. It was abuse perpetrated by a misguided, manipulative and dangerous man, tragically playing on the longing of his young victims to live godly lives."[4] But that was not

1. Jones, cited in *Inquiry into Chichester Diocese*, 15.
2. Ahmari, *From Fire by Water*.
3. Jenkins, "Road from Damascus."
4. Bishop Andrew Watson, cited in Sherwood, "C of E Bishop."

how Smyth saw it. He thought he was doing God's will in administering the fatherly discipline called for in biblical texts that he liked to recite, including Luke 12:47: "And that servant who knew his master's will, but did not make ready or act according to his will, shall receive a severe beating." The Ruston Report written by fellow Christian leaders in response to growing concerns about Smyth and his supporters noted that: "The motives were always seen as good by operators and participants—the sanctifying of young Christian men and the blessings of fatherly discipline . . . Prayer, praise and loving concern in Christ's name were evident at every point."[5]

Well-meaning friends of religion contribute to the problem of splitting when, faced by abuses of spiritual power, they insist that this is not real religion. The word *Islamism* has been invented to maintain the distinction between false religion and true. The assumption is that Islam, like the other Abrahamic religions, is innocent and good, and that it is only a few rotten apples who give it a bad name. But there is no pure and innocent core to any religion, and no teaching or theology that issues infallibly in just and loving acts.

Idealizing tendencies in religious thinking help to explain one of the most puzzling aspects of the scandal over clerical abuse and cover-up: why, after such a thorough exposure of the problem since the 1990s, the same patterns of behavior have been repeated again and again right down to the present day. When Philip Jenkins published *Pedophiles and Priests* in 2001, he predicted that the scandal that had engulfed the Catholic Church was nearing its end, but decades later more stories are still emerging, not just in the Catholic Church but in other churches, too. In England, the Catholic boarding school at Ampleforth ignored so many demands to improve safeguarding that the Charity Commission had to step in to take over responsibility for protecting children.[6] Such refusal to take action is so egregious and the risks involved so great, that explaining the failure solely in terms of a concern about reputation is not sufficient. A missing observation is that persistent abuse was covered up even after the facts were exposed because, in the thinking of enough of those in charge, abusive monks and priests must, by virtue of their calling and office, be spiritual and good. In other words, what is being defended is not only external reputation but deeply

---

5. A report on Smyth written by fellow leaders at the Bible camps where he operated. Cited in Scott, "Beating Posh Boys for Jesus."

6. Sherwood, "Top Catholic School."

internalized, idealized ideas about the higher, untouchable status of those specially chosen by the one true God.

The public inquiries into the abuse of children reveal too many powerful people in Anglican, Catholic, and other churches who have elevated themselves, in their own minds and teachings, above the failings and safeguards that apply to the rest of society. Alienation from the modern "secular" world has grown amongst church leaders as their influence has declined. Some go so far as to celebrate secularization as a cleansing process that leaves a faithful remnant witnessing to God and speaking truth to what some Catholic leaders call a "culture of death."

The popular American writer Rod Dreher argues that only an alternative civilization—"the Benedict option"—can now save the Christian faith. This means "making monasteries, of a sort, of our homes and hearts, [that] we may develop the spiritual disciplines necessary to endure this seemingly endless trial and to keep the light of faith burning brightly amid this new Dark Age."[7] This is the same sort of idea that Alasdair MacIntyre espoused in *After Virtue*, and which was been seized on by many "postliberal" theologians. It should give pause for thought that Benedictine communities have been exposed as being some of the very worst institutions for abuse of children and for cover-up.

Reinhold Niebuhr's *Christ and Culture*, originally published in 1951, set a dangerous precedent when it talked about "Christ" and "culture" as if they were separate things. This idea was taken over uncritically in many Christian circles, and the term "culture Christians" became an insult. The error here is to assume that a faith with no connection to culture is possible, let alone desirable. It is a persistent fantasy that afflicts all religions that there can be a cleansing mission that will strip away "culture" and leave only the gleaming raiments of (our) pure religion. A fundamentalist Christian cult that operates at the highest levels of American society talks about their allegiance to "Jesus plus nothing."[8] But there is no escape from culture, even in a monastery, and those who attempt this impossibility usually end up with a worse kind of culture than the one they were trying to escape from, because they are oblivious to its flaws and dangerously defensive. "Faith," said Wilfred Cantwell Smith, "lies beyond theology, in the hearts of men. Truth lies beyond faith, in the heart of God."[9] Even if this is true, we can

---

7. Dreher, "What Must Survive."

8. Sharlet, *Family*, 58.

9. Smith, *Meaning and End of Religion*, 167.

never be sure that we have got there. Therefore we must take responsibility even for the God/s we feel sure are speaking to us in the depths of our own collective or personal experience.

There is an inhibiting pious fear that such a critical spirit is idolatrous and unfaithful. God and holy Scriptures must judge us, not the other way about. Karl Barth's stirring words about idolatry have proved lastingly influential. "When the church proclaims God's revelation," he says, "it reads and explains the Word . . . It is, and remains grateful for the knowledge of God in which he has given himself to us by giving up his Son."[10] But "revelation" and "the Word" are dangerously elusive concepts that too easily end up meaning "my version of orthodoxy." It is possible to admire the way that Barth resisted Nazi ideology without accepting how he deployed "revelation" to uphold his Calvinistic version of Christianity against all the rest. The Barthian legacy needs to be assessed not only in relation to fascism, but in relation to the way it can be used to disguise thought control and other abuses of power.

The desire to retreat to a place of sanctuary is understandable. Experiences of God/s touch the soul, so there is a need to defend religious freedom. But because religion is so important, it is also consequential— not just for me but for those whose lives I, or my community, may touch. It is helpful to remember that our God/s come to us swirled up with a host of very human associations and blind spots. They create us and we create them. Because we exist in symbiosis with our God/s, we must take responsibility for them, as well as for the institutional arrangements of the religions of which they are part. As with so many things, it is always helpful to ask: who is getting what out of this?

10. Barth, *Church Dogmatics* II/1, 178.

4. THEOLOGY AS AUTOBIOGRAPHY

NPH

WHAT IS CHRISTIANITY? THEOLOGIANS and church leaders continue to give ready answers to this question. But if these answers are set alongside one another, or against the claims and emphases of earlier generations of Christians, startling differences declare themselves. Attempts are sometimes made to resolve contradictions by appeal to the idea of development, but one person's development is another's departure from the pristine ideal. In any case notions of development depend on a selective reconstruction of our past to ensure that it conforms to what we judge appropriate in the present. In reality Christianity is constantly taking different forms in the light of present experience and aspiration. The appeal to tradition can conceal and distract from a quite different agenda.

The earliest Christians to leave information about themselves believed that their faith originated with a group of disciples, who had lost their leader. But that was then, a long time ago and in a distant place. How we get from there and then to here and now is a historian's question, opening on vistas of fascinating complexity. But any answer reached by this route to the question "What is Christianity?" is likely to be "A thousand different things." Historical study reveals a remarkable diversity of beliefs and practices, while observation of the contemporary scene shows comparable variety.

It might well be answered that our foundation is a revealed truth that transcends all times and places. This means that the only satisfying answer is a theological one. History says what it can, but theology offers the authoritative word. But if theology is a commentary on what is happening—and it cannot be less than that—it will not yield such timeless truths and universal moral positions as the proponents of a transcultural and transhistorical theology imagine. The theological project is, rather, autobiographical. It is the task of reflecting on the befores and afters of that part of the process of revision to which I am able to bear witness because I am part of it. This project will touch on historical, social, psychological, economic, and political matters, for all these are inescapably involved in any serious treatment of the world we share.

A cautionary word comes from the post-Freudian psychoanalyst Adam Phillips, to the effect that autobiography is a cover story. It must be so because it is a particular construction of the past, and as such denies other possible constructions. What at any time I want to call the story of my life is in fact only one of many possible versions, or one story out of the many that I am living. Phillips's observation is salutary in raising the question of what my autobiography is unconsciously denying or excluding. The conclusion is not to abandon autobiography but to recognize that whatever emerges cannot be the whole story and needs critical questioning, not least by the autobiographer. This version cries out for other versions, there being no such thing as the whole story. We are in any case writing from the inside, with the consequence that the viewpoint taken cannot avoid partiality.

Meanwhile those who so readily stigmatize what they call subjectivism in our culture seem to suppose that an unfiltered objectivity is available, known in theological terms as orthodoxy. According to this view revelation, located primarily either in the Bible or in the church, gives the individual ready access, without further mediation, to the truths of faith. We are thus seen as passive recipients of authoritative texts, an image which blinds us to the many and varied ways in which we are makers of them. In *Is There a Text in This Class?* Stanley Fish takes the example of Augustine, who thinks he is interpreting a scriptural text when in fact he has already decided what the meaning must be: everything in the Bible is about the love of God.[1] This turns out to be the same meaning that he thinks he finds in the other texts. In other words, it is the community that is creating the text, not the other way round. Orthodoxy cannot be more than that which prevails in a particular group at a particular time. Christians unsympathetic to this point of view tend to say that it amounts to claiming that the only truth is what my group declares to be true. This is a gross caricature, for it is compatible with what Fish is saying to acknowledge that interpretation is not the activity of enclosed interpretative communities but takes place within a wider human context.

1. Fish, *Is There a Text in This Class?*, 170.

The argument in the previous paragraphs began with the individual and ended with the group, which might appear a sleight of hand. But the implied antithesis is false, for even at our most eremitical we are each part of a community. Autobiography is the product not of an isolated individual but of a culture. It is part of an ongoing conversation, the possibility of which presupposes a context for such communication. My autobiography is part of the community's text-making and cannot be understood apart from that process. It is important to note that this fact does not condemn us to mere repetition of a common mind. The content is not predetermined, and autobiography can broach new horizons, giving others permission to think their story differently from hitherto.

What then of those doctrines commonly supposed to form the indispensable core of Christian faith? Do they not have an objectivity that puts them outside the otherwise endless, and endlessly inconclusive, processes of text-making? In an unpublished essay the theologian Sebastian Moore likened classical doctrinal formulae to the lava that remains after a volcanic eruption. They are solidified traces of a transformative experience. The mistake is to suppose that allegiance to the doctrines gives, or can do duty for, the experience that they articulate. To allow credal and catechetical formulations to occupy the foreground, to insist on formal allegiance to them as the sine qua non of faith, is to displace present experience and its possibilities in the name of an alleged revelation that is only a fossilized version of elements in our past. Again the autobiographical note is inescapable.

The themes a particular theologian chooses to explore are not plucked out of the air. They are chosen because he or she is in one way or another preoccupied by them, so that in this sense at least doctrines are part of our biographies. Why, for instance, did I come to have a lively interest in Christian teaching about, and attitudes to, death and resurrection, which led to my first book? Because someone of whom I was a disciple, upon whose every word I hung, had suddenly taken his own life. In the face of this shocking and potentially scandalizing event I wanted to vindicate him, and of course my own allegiance to his ideas. But this agenda was not acknowledged at the time, and indeed was not fully conscious. What came across was a strong defense of a particular form of resurrection-faith, couched in terms of exclusivist claims for Jesus to which I no longer subscribe. Such claims characterize a great deal of modern Christian thinking. There is a tendency among theologians to speak of the divine-human relationship as definitively completed in Jesus Christ. It must be asked what function these claims are performing in the lives of those theologians who continue to propound them in the face of a new sensitivity to other faiths and none.

It is fashionable among some Christians to speak of "the gospel story." In reality what we have is four Gospels; and subsequent versions of Jesus, artistic as well as literary, so many and various as to be uncountable. We can always get one story out of a group of stories; but what we get will always be another story. The "gospel story" brigade are privileging one highly selective version, insisting that this is the story. Why the observable diversity is so readily minimized by so many in a position to know better is a more elusive question, which may relate to power games and a need to have a clear Christian identity.

The work of those scholars who seriously pursue the question of the historical Jesus exemplifies Phillips's point about a cover story. Their careful constructions, often based on meticulous research, succeed only in producing a lifeless figure. Who is bothered about Ed Sanders's Jesus, or Gerd Theissen's Jesus, or Tom Wright's Jesus? Even if these versions are accurate as far as they go, they do not put us in touch with a living person. What is going wrong? It is not that there is conscious falsification. It is rather that the unacceptable has been either excluded or included in a tamed form. Freud once told someone who said he was not much interested in himself: "You have made everything so clear that it doesn't interest me either." In other words, a person whose self-presentation is completely coherent is acknowledging only what is trivial, and so avoiding everything of interest about him or herself. In the same conversation Freud insisted that clarity is superficial, a bold assertion but one which theology needs to take very seriously. Attempts to present Jesus as completely transparent encounter the same limitation: too much is missing, or subdued, for the venture to be compelling. It is not that these scholars, or anyone else, set out to idealize Jesus, but rather that in this genre only the idealized is intelligible.

If it is suggested that the problem is a lack of information about Jesus the answer is that, on the contrary, more information from the storyteller would be more cover story. Freud would not have been interested in more information from his interlocutor, for that would have been merely more of the same. In the case of Jesus there seems no alternative to acceptance that we know very little about him. In the course of Christian history a very great range of images, ideas, and aspirations have been projected onto the figure of Jesus; nor is contemporary Christianity untouched by this process. If theology is autobiography, stories of our projections and their withdrawal must be told, although the process is not always easy to spot. If such a telling is not attempted we shall be operating either in ideological or mystical mode, without the necessary hermeneutic of suspicion.

5. CHRISTIAN MORALITY?

NPH

HAVING BEEN REARED ON and given allegiance to a morality that claimed to be rigorous, comprehensive, and distinctively Christian, I have spent at least the last thirty years unlearning this in the light of experience and observation. The morality of my youth now appears as an ethics of boundaries rather than of transformation.

In the dissolution of this seemingly watertight moral system, conversation, thinking, reading, and the task of teaching ethics to prospective clergy have all played their part, but the touchstone is observation of what goes on in people's lives. The notion of theology in play, whether or not labeled as pastoral, is essentially that of a reflection on what is happening. From this point of view there is no need to establish connections between theology and ethics, since there can be no separation.

People sometimes ask: "Where does God come in?" The question is based on a misunderstanding; for what is happening is, if anywhere, the place of God. The past is important only because it has happened, and the future is not yet revealed. The present contains the past and invites the future: all three are inseparable and in a sense indistinguishable. If some sense of the mystery of all things does not burgeon for us in the processes in which we find ourselves involved, then attempts to bring God in or to find God elsewhere are in vain. The mystical tradition is wise to speak of the sacrament of the present moment: that is all we have, that is the gift and the opportunity, that is where possibilities are recognized and embraced—or not.

It is commonly assumed within and outside the church that Christian teaching on moral fundamentals has always been the same. It is also usually supposed that these alleged fundamentals are distinctive, being derived from or at least in some sense guided by the moral teachings of the Bible. None of these assumptions can survive critical scrutiny. The Bible is not a book but a library, its components written from cultural and religious standpoints differing in important ways from each other and from current concerns.

In the case of the Jewish Scriptures it is easy not to notice that some of the most important figures are in our terms morally reprehensible. Abraham, praised as our father in faith, heard the Lord's command to kill his son and set out to obey. At the level of the application of principles there is no difference between this state of mind and the response of Peter Sutcliffe, popularly known as the Yorkshire Ripper, to angelic voices telling him to kill prostitutes. (Kierkegaard, for whom ethics meant an ethics of principles, described Abraham's response as involving the suspension of ethics.[1]) Jacob, whose God Christians claim to worship, deceived his blind father in order to cheat his elder brother out of his inheritance. This deceit is a key moment in his rise to a highly honored role in the tradition. Whatever we are expected to learn from these stories, it is not what is ordinarily called morality.

Then there is Joshua's jihad to exterminate the inhabitants of Palestine, making way for the Israelites. This story, including its racist and religiously intolerant use at times in the past, is dealt with by modern Christians largely by pretending it is not there. This denial is only the most spectacular example of the vain but persistent attempt to homogenize the Bible in the light of currently dominant convictions and concerns. Such attempted homogenization is necessary as long as the traditional claim is made that everything in the Bible is the revealed word of God for all times and places.

What then of Jesus? Our sources do not corroborate the common picture of him as an outstanding moral teacher and exemplar. The texts present him as involved in a fierce ongoing struggle about the religious identity and future of Israel. This seems to have included an intense dialectic with his theological enemies about the purpose and limitations of the Torah. The Hebrew word *torah*, commonly and misleadingly translated as law, has to do with the particular history and self-understanding of the Jewish people. The Torah, including the Ten Commandments, is not a universal code or set of principles or values. There is therefore no reason to suppose Jesus was a moral reformer, still less a personification of the virtues. Indeed these are sometimes flouted by him in the story as we have it. Two examples, one from his teaching and the other from his life, may help.

He insists on hatred of close relatives as a necessary condition of discipleship. True, another source has him referring to the commandment to

---

1. Kierkegaard, *Fear and Trembling*, 83–95.

honor parents, but the commentators' tendency to minimize and distance the "hard saying" in favor of this generally accepted maxim is to be resisted.[2]

The second example: Jesus put himself in line for his own death by setting his face towards Jerusalem, the place of the killing of the prophets. Retrospectively, a theology emerged that enabled his followers to acclaim this as a supreme act of love. But it is part of the story that his execution under a curse outside the city wall was seen by the disciples as a letdown, a desertion of them, a cruel undermining of the hope he had aroused in them. A martyr, or indeed a hero of the revolution, dies for a recognizable cause. Despite modern attempts to say that he died in the cause of justice or freedom, no moral category can accommodate, much less commend, Jesus' approach to his death, which remains unexplained. It approximates to that of a suicide. This scandal is at the heart of the story.[3]

Christians tend to cheat by arguing that it was all in accord with a divine design to which Jesus alone had access. But this is to take away the contingency and consequent unpredictability of the events which made up the Passion. Those events, thus accounted for, cease to be the kind of happenings with which we find ourselves engaged. The appeal to an omniscient God who always knows in advance what is going to happen removes human responsibility. Deprived of such a crutch, Jesus' story comes alive. It is not so much a question of finding this story directly useful or helpful, as of finding ourselves in the story. But this does not work at appropriate depth unless we identify with all the characters. Only moralistic reductionism can produce from this material a tale of goodies and baddies. Insofar as these texts remain alive for us their interest and power lie elsewhere. A living text, it has been said, is always giving birth to meanings. While the story of Jesus provides part of the context for our decision-making, we have to take responsibility not only for our actions but for our interpretation of the story.

In the earliest manifestations known to us, Christianity was not characterized by a distinctive approach to morality. For example, the lists of vices in the letters attributed to Paul are largely conventional, products of the milieu in which Christianity came to birth. These letters sometimes go out of their way to stress the moral respectability of Christian behavior. Notice for instance the stress on the importance of obedience to the magistrate, and of wives and slaves to their husbands and masters.

2. Harvey, *Morals of Jesus,* 58.

3. Harvey, *Death's Gift,* 75–82.

Modern Christians tend to speak as if what is distinctive about their morality is that it is rooted in a love which originates with Jesus. But the Gospel material about the life and teaching of Jesus, manifesting as it does a wonderful array of multiple creative ambiguities, does not directly advance understanding of the meaning and practice of love. As for Paul, those remarks in which he reinterprets the Torah in terms of the command to love can offer us no moral guidance, for our struggle is not with the Torah. Furthermore, his often-quoted hymn to love is a description of some of the best in human behavior. Turned into prescriptions, this becomes either unhelpful or dangerous. The claim, whether ancient or modern, that love is what morality is all about is of no help in problematic situations. In *Christian Morality: The Word Becomes Flesh,* Josef Fuchs offered the at first sight surprising suggestion that the moral task can be properly defined as self-realization, provided that reductionist concepts of the self are avoided.

What about the Sermon on the Mount? Some Christians have doubtless been deeply influenced in their attitude to morality by particular sentences from this collection, but as a whole it has never formed the basis of any systematic or sustained thinking about morals. Luther thought it represented an unlivable ideal, the function of which was to convince us of our need for divine forgiveness. Some of his medieval predecessors held that the sermon consisted of "counsels of perfection" for a spiritual elite. The fact that such tortuous interpretations arose within the Christian mainstream indicates the recalcitrance of this material to being treated as a primary text for Christian ethics.

Can the idea of an essence of Christian morality be saved by some concept of development? On the contrary, talk of development prevents a straight look at the history of Christian thinking about morality. Much assimilation from surrounding cultures has occurred, as in the rise of theories of natural law and of virtue and character, now enjoying a revival. Distinctively modern emphases found in Western Christianity were developed outside the Christian mainstream. These include doctrines of human rights and of religious liberty, both once anathema to the church. There are also what might loosely be called existentialist approaches, with a strong stress on authentic individual choice as the constitutive factor in moral living.

Some Christian groupings resist this eclecticism in the name of revealed truth, some appealing to the Bible, others to tradition. They identify Christian faith with absolutist answers to particular moral questions. These attempts are not as innocent as might be supposed, relying on philosophical assumptions that are taken for granted and depending on a selective use and questionable hermeneutic of traditional texts. These groups could well be asked whether their underlying agenda is the maintenance of a distinctive Christian identity against the perceived inroads of modernity. In other words, is their moral program pursued not so much for its own sake as for its function of securing a threatened Christian identity? This has certainly happened repeatedly in the past, when moral questions became entangled in attempts to secure boundaries. Ambrose of Milan is a case in point. He gave priority in the Christian moral order to consecrated virginity because he saw consecrated female virgins, with their high symbolic and liturgical visibility, as "boundary stones" of the church.[4]

The phrase "justice and peace" looms large in some contemporary Christian discourses. In the course of history, the church has validated imperial, feudal, and egalitarian political systems, including of course slavery, serfdom, and antisemitism. While it is true that tyrannies of various kinds, from Roman imperialism onwards, have been criticized and even resisted by some Christians, the record of Christian political thinking and practice is from the beginning very mixed. It has been suggested that the New Testament books were written by those in the ascendancy in the church who interpreted Jesus in ways that played down his subversive thrust. But it is an illusion to suppose that we can go back behind these diverse and fragmentary texts to establish some certainty about the real, pure Jesus. What we have is a tradition, which offers and allows a variety of interpretations. We lack unmediated access to Jesus.[5]

Appeals to the Trinity as a model of how humans should relate to one another in the political order were fashionable recently. It was forgotten that the same doctrine was earlier used with equal sincerity to offer theocratic legitimacy to a hierarchical society. What is happening here is the projection of a preferred notion of the political order onto the doctrine of the Trinity. In any case the forms of justice being so strongly advocated by Christians are characteristic of some of the idealistic political aspirations of their times, and cannot be claimed as a distinctively Christian venture.

As to peace, Christians have held almost every conceivable outlook from outright pacifism (claimed to originate with Jesus) via the just war theory to the Crusading spirit. There is also the suggestion that the peace

4. Brown, *Body and Society,* 356.

5. See Parker, *Living Text of the Gospels,* and Fowl, "Quest of the Historical Jesus."

of which Jesus speaks has no direct bearing on the external order or on the particulars of behavior, but is instead a state of inner harmony with God in all circumstances. Given this range of divergent ways of seeking to follow the tradition it is not at all clear what Christians mean by peace, still less whether the word has any distinctively Christian resonance.[6]

These examples could be multiplied. They are chosen to illustrate the fact that there is not, and never has been, a Christian consensus on moral matters. Whatever resources may be available in the various Christian traditions, they are not of such a kind as to make it possible to speak of a Christian basis for morality. The current insistence of some Christian leaders and thinkers on a single point of view, especially though not exclusively on aspects of medical and sexual ethics, cannot alter the fact that there are profound disagreements within all the churches on these and all other moral questions. The widespread assumption that there is some kind of claim to moral unanimity among Christians, at least on fundamentals, recurs, and prevents healthy debate.

It has been argued that the resurrection of Jesus from the dead is the key to Christian morality.[7] Part of this thesis is that the resurrection vindicates what is called "the created order," in which appropriate patterns of relationship are laid down. The moral task then becomes conformity to the original order. We are supposed to find a revealed description of this order in the opening chapters of Genesis. As with a morality of natural law, this tends in practice to be conservative of those patterns of relating that are familiar at the time and which are all too easily equated with what is thought to be transcultural and transhistorical. In an age when we are being sensitized to the fact that particular forms of human relationship are at least in part social constructions, proponents of "the created order" insist that there is an unchanging pattern to human living and relating, from which everything else is a falling short.

An obvious case in point is marriage, which has meant and continues to mean different things in different times and places. The attempt to treat it as a univocal term, and as an institution uniquely privileged by God, is an idealization with an oppressive function. It may be argued against this that while the practice is messy and various we must retain allegiance to marriage as an ideal form, for without this there is no basis for criticizing changing patterns of relating. On the contrary, talk of fidelity in

---

6. Hauerwas, in *Peaceable Kingdom*, expresses an opposing view.

7. For example, by O'Donovan, in *Resurrection and Moral Order*.

difficulties may obfuscate the power play proceeding in the relationship, usually though not invariably to the detriment of the woman. In all these ways the invocation of Christian faith to keep the ideal in business militates against clear-sighted analysis and responsible action.

Attention to the ideal distracts from properly critical attention to the forms of relationship that are proceeding among us. The insistent sacralizing of marriage marginalizes other possible forms of relationship. Two examples follow. A common defense of remarriage after divorce is that it is a second attempt at what marriage is supposed to be.[8] This fails to respect the first marriage, since it entails saying either that it was not a real marriage or that the earlier relationship has no enduring significance. The critical question is: in what ways can the first marriage be recognized and valued within the second? This requires accepting that a second marriage is not the same kind of thing as the first, but that both can be equally valid as forms of relationship. A second example is that of same-sex partnerships, the commonest defense of which is that they can approximate to the ideal of marriage. This fails to take seriously the variety of same-sex relationships that occur, and their possible differences from heterosexual relationships. The question is not whether a gay or lesbian relationship conforms to an ideal transposed from the heterosexual context, but whether it is oppressive or liberating for those involved.[9] Concentrating on the ideal of lifelong partnership also overlooks the obvious fact that same-sex friendships with an erotic dimension are sometimes, though by no means always, part of psychosexual development.

The point made in the previous paragraph about oppression and liberation has much wider bearings. Across the whole spectrum of sexual relationships other than marriage, the question, "Who is getting what out of this?" opens up a more penetrating line of enquiry than questions of conformity or otherwise to an ideal. (This insight comes from an unpublished presentation by Grace M. Jantzen on her role as ethicist in the Canadian government's Royal Commission on surrogate motherhood. She began with what she later saw as a conventional human rights approach, but soon came to see that the question of who is getting what out of this provoked a deeper and more accurate analysis.) This question cuts deeper on a wider front than an uncritical appeal to human rights.

---

8. See, for example, Kelly, *Divorce and Second Marriage,* 8.

9. Stuart, *Just Good Friends,* 9.

An odd feature of most theological work on morality is its innocence of the idea of evolution and of the power of the unconscious mind. There is something surreal about a conversation purporting to address the fundamentals of behavior that proceeds as if we lived in a pre-evolutionary and pre-Freudian world. The churches have in practice long since adopted the Enlightenment's assumption that what defines us all, except perhaps those classified as mad, is a core of rationality. This presupposition is also shared by many theologians who see themselves as attacking the Enlightenment. It has led to simplistic and overly individualistic notions of free will as the source of human actions. Recognition of the extent to which the unconscious can dictate individual and corporate behavior gravely threatens such moralistic notions; but the churches, in common with one strand in our culture, have difficulty in hoisting in this very different perception of what often drives our behavior. Meanwhile evolution's suggestion that life spontaneously takes new forms in response to changing circumstances undermines a morality of static essences and self-conscious virtue. Too great an insistence on an ideal in any aspect of life, not least in a religious context, can militate against moral development, with destructive consequences.

Nothing said so far need be taken to mean that there are no Christian resources available that bear on behavior. It is unfortunate that the contemporary revival of interest in virtue and character largely presupposes that the classical notions sit comfortably with the theological virtues. There is a baneful confusion here, for faith, hope, and love are not about virtue and character in the classical sense at all. They do not demand an understanding of humankind as essentially rational. The character they are liable to form is unlikely to fit with the norms of prudence, justice, fortitude, and temperance. The classical virtues assume we know what the good life is; the theological virtues do not. Whereas the former are acquired by education, the latter are seen as gifts.

Faith, hope, and love are not, of course, confined to Christianity. But they connect with the story of Jesus, which, as has already been argued, is not a moral tale. For as long as this story continues to be told, it will influence our behavior. It does so by way of interaction between elements in it and what is happening in our lives and in our world. Faith, meaning trust in awareness, is the key. The heart of faith is a disciplined wakefulness, a clear-eyed attentiveness to what is going on rather than a prior allegiance to a set of beliefs and practices. If morality in the form of universal principles or imperatives is to hold sway there is no place for faith, for morality has become God. A living faith is liable to insist on quite other and less readily intelligible priorities, which are none the less urgent and taxing for that.

The critic who says that an ethics of transformation provides no viable alternative to an ethics of principles or values is missing the point. From the angle of faith the latter kind of morality has no substance other than as an instrument of social control. The insistence on a supplement to faith in the form of principles or values is a demand for a security mechanism. If it is possible to speak at all of a Christian morality it is a morality of gift and call.[10] The theological virtues of faith, hope, and love remain to be worked out in fear and trembling.

10. See McDonagh, *Gift and Call.*

6. THE EXPERIENCE OF EXCLUSION

LW

A FRIEND PROPOSES THAT the world can be divided into those who know what it is to be excluded and those who do not. Not total exclusion, for one would hardly care about that with which one has no connection: no, the semi-exclusion of looking through a door but being barred entry. That is the exclusion that hurts and haunts; it can become life-defining if you let it.

Some of us will remember the childhood experience of creeping out of bed to listen to the murmur of adults gathering for a party downstairs. That is an experience of exclusion, but in some ways a delicious one. The child is barred from participation by virtue of their tender years, but knows a mixture of frustration and excitement in the contemplation of a world that will one day be opened to them: a kingdom waiting to be conquered.

My earliest memory of exclusion had less by way of compensation. I must have been around six years old when my grandfather took me to the officers' mess at his regimental HQ. I cannot remember why, but I suspect he had been left to babysit and wanted a drink. I can remember the flock wallpaper, the gilt-framed pictures, the jewel-like bottles behind the bar. Men would salute and smile. Their ease derived from knowledge of their position. No doubt I idealized the situation. But from that day on I fantasized about being a soldier—until I learned that the option was closed to me, for in those days women were confined to lower ranks and occupations and made to wear skirts and heels.

For those who dwell at the center of things, their reality is how things are, and their identity does not have to be defended. For outsiders, it can never be like that. They often grow up with a nagging and shameful sense of being ill-fitting and inadequate. Whether because of race, ethnicity, gender, class, or other things, the world is not theirs and they are there on sufferance rather than in their own right. They should be grateful. Even for outsiders who manage to make their way in, so much energy must be invested in proving themselves that there is often little left over, while "making it" may prove a mixed blessing.

I have met many people who feel a sense of exclusion from "their" church. I am one of them. As a young woman I thought I belonged. It was a shock to find out that they did not want me or, to be accurate, wanted me only in an edited form. As a young tutor in an Anglican training college I used to be sent to the railway station to chauffeur visiting preachers back to college. I would deliver them to the principal's study and the door would be shut in my face. It was a perfect metaphor for women's position in the Church of England in the early 1990s and it left me with a question that I couldn't face at the time: can you, should you, embrace what excludes you?

Luke Babb, a gay man who parted ways with his church in the USA "on terms too unkind" for him ever to wish to return, writes of the continuing pull it has for him, even though latterly he has been sustained by paganism: "I go to churches because I have no holy spaces of my own."[1] Standing in front of a statue of the goddess Aphrodite in the British Museum one day, he wants to worship her but is inhibited by the setting. He speaks of the moment as one of "recognition, of being somewhere holy . . . taken from its context and realigned" and longs for the chance to sing and praise in a public setting, as he used to do in church.[2]

Sometimes I also miss worshipping ancestral gods in the company of others who love them too. I try going to church, but the sense of exclusion gets in the way. I see it as a symptom of something bigger—an alienation that is widely shared but takes many forms. Sometimes it is manifest as atheism, sometimes as an unresolved attitude to the churches: many people want them to exist but don't want anything to do with them.

Matthew, a victim of clerical abuse who was once a priest himself, tells me that "It's done me good to stand back [from the church]. I used to say mass from a book in front of me, but the more I examine what I once said and often taught by rote —'a once for all and sufficient sacrifice,' the more I realize a lot of it was habit. Indoctrination almost. So maybe my

1. Babb, "Sacred Space."
2. Babb, "Sacred Space."

abuse has been my saving."[3] He talks about friendships he has found in other places, with dogs as well as people.

Luke Babb talks about "stumbling back to the homes of the gods" after his exile from church.[4] Some exiles will never feel the same sense of inclusion that they once felt in church. Perhaps that is fine. Perhaps the painful sense of being driven out of home was a necessary part of growing up. We had to give up the fantasy of belonging to a "family" in which we were safe and loved. That is too much expectation for any institution to bear, and those that are most eager to promise it should be treated with caution.

3. Woodhead, "Rape Followed by Bureaucracy," 99.
4. Babb, "Sacred Space."

7. LOVE ISN'T ALL YOU NEED

LW

WISDOM, ACCORDING TO THE book of Proverbs, "cries aloud in the street; in the markets she raises her voice; on the top of the walls she cries out; at the entrance of the city gates she speaks" (Proverbs 1:20). Translating for today, we could say that wisdom can be found at the hairdresser or the supermarket—and if this is true of wisdom, it is surely true of love, too. You don't need a theology degree or an ordination certificate to know love or show it. So why are Christians so ready to claim a special ownership?

In the middle of a service video-streamed from his kitchen at the start of the coronavirus pandemic, Archbishop Justin Welby described love as a "Christian distinctive." It struck a jarring note. What could it mean? Did he mean that Christians are distinctively loving? More so than the frontline health workers struggling to save lives? How odd that sounds to victims of abuse in the Church of England who await apology and reparation. So let us assume that the archbishop did not mean his remark to be taken in this way.

Perhaps Justin Welby meant that Christians are distinctively loving compared to followers of other religions. Because he committed to interfaith dialogue and reconciliation, this seems a risky thing to say. In any case, how could anyone possibly judge? Even the most overreaching scientist has not yet come up with a love measurement, so far as I know. It is true that church leaders have a tendency to labor the good works of the churches—foodbanks, homeless shelters, and loving communities—while taking swipes at the heartless and uncaring nature of "secular" society. Religion is a competitive business and there is pressure to be distinctive in an age of marketing, competing, and winning. Fair enough. Churches have stipends to pay and face to save. But it has zero to do with love.

I think the most likely interpretation is that the archbishop was making an unthinking identity claim that is rooted in a theology that maintains that Christianity is a religion of love not law, its God the God of Love par excellence. "See what love [these Christians] bear toward each other!" said Tertullian in the late second century, and that boast is still regularly repeated.[1]

There are numerous attempts to define "Christian love" in a way that sets it apart from the everyday love of the marketplace. In the mid-twentieth century, the theologian Anders Nygren and the popular Christian writer C.S. Lewis both wrote influential books distinguishing "eros"—passionate, self-interested, desiring, and worldly love—from "agape"—disinterested, benevolent, sacrificial, and properly Christian love.[2] Both celebrated Jesus as the perfect exemplar of agape, the face of divine love. In this approach, the crucifixion is central: it is where God's saving work is performed, where salvation history finds its turning point, and where love is uniquely revealed. Resurrection becomes proof.

Lurking behind the archbishop's remark about love, then, is a whole edifice of theological interpretation that colors "Christian love" with ideas of self-sacrifice and extreme suffering and makes it into something unique. I will not rehearse all the objections, including the vital observation that the contrast between Christian love and Jewish law is bound up with antisemitism. My objections come from a more personal place.

In a Catholic convent school I attended for a few years, life-size statues of Jesus hung on the classroom walls, looking down on us reproachfully as we went about our trivial and self-interested pursuits. When, in my village church, we sang hymns like Isaac Watts's "When I Survey the Wondrous Cross," I took seriously the line that says God "demands my soul, my life, my all." We absorbed the belief that we must crush our own desires in order to be closer to Jesus. This reinforced a wider message that children should be "seen and not heard" and never "answer back" or "show off." Looking back, I see how much it cost me. It denied me the vocabulary, confidence, and rationale to stop others from taking advantage in small ways or large—or even to register when it was happening. A guilt-inducing self-sacrificial ethic made me discount my actual feelings in favor of the loving kindness I "should" be feeling, so that I lost the ability to pick up early warning signals in abusive situations. It left no capacity for "this doesn't feel right" or "I deserve better."

1. Tertullian, *Apologeticum,* 39, section 7. Cited by MacMullen, *Christianizing,* 92, who also notes that it is "often quoted."

2. Nygren, *Agape and Eros*; Lewis, *Four Loves.*

Sacrificial love also became a cover for power games of a perverse kind. As children we picked up the implicit message that self-effacement brought reward. To sacrifice one's strongest desires might give control over self and situation—part of the logic of anorexia and related disorders—and enhance the power of whatever ideal one served. The greater the act of will and the greater the desire overcome, the greater the power. Asceticism is not always benign. In sacrificing to a higher power, whether cause, institution, or God, that power is enhanced, and with it my own. An all-powerful God demands the sacrifice of the self and the sacrifice of the self renders God all-powerful. If the blood of the martyrs was the seed of the church, that was partly because their sacrifice convinced some contemporaries that the church's God was more powerful than pagan gods who received only animal sacrifice. God fills up the space vacated by the dismembered bodies of the dead. This gives dynamism to an ethic of self-sacrifice in which for God to be everything we must become nothing. This hungry-God's followers, having renounced power, can let it in again by the back door, presenting themselves as the servants of God, and hiding the power drive.

It was feminism that first raised serious questions about the self-sacrificial love ethic in my mind. Feminist theologians unpicked a tangle of assumptions and considered their outcomes. Some pointed out how an ethic of selfless love could leave women incapable of establishing a confident, defensible self. Others wrote about the uneven social distribution of the emotional burden of sin.[3] Some sent out early warnings about abuse, as biblical scholars dissected "texts of terror" that speak freely of the rape and murder of women.[4] I absorbed all this with a sense of grateful recognition.

When I left home and college to pursue a career, the limitations of the self-sacrificial "agape" ethic became even clearer. Many young women of my generation faced the option of withdrawing back to cocoons of (hoped for) domestic loving kindness, or reconstructing our identities and ethics to cope with the male-dominated worlds we entered, in which sacrificial love was clearly not enough. Gradually, my ideas about love and its all-sufficiency changed.

I saw that theological definitions of love—like "one-way sacrificial benevolence"—act like blinders on a horse. We see love only where we are directed to look. But Jesus says, "nor will they say, 'Lo, here it is!' or

---

3. For example, Saiving-Goldstein, "Feminine View," and Woodhead, "Love and Justice."

4. Trible, *Texts of Terror.*

'There!' For behold, the kingdom of God is in the midst of you" (Luke: 17:21). He points to love and faith in the last places people thought to look—among sex workers and tax collectors. If our gaze is fixed only on an atoning savior on a cross, or a Mother Theresa, we overlook other kinds of love. If we build self-giving love into our sense of who we "distinctively" are, it may be very hard indeed to admit to any darkness within: acts of cruelty get covered up. Claiming a special connection to love can be a way of covering over feelings of inadequacy and shame—going round them rather than through them in order to be worthy.

Jesus' own motives remain hidden from us. The New Testament is a compendium of different interpretations of his life, death, and resurrection, to which subsequent tradition adds many more. Sacrificial love is just one key to reading the texts, but it has been pushed so hard that it is often difficult to see the other meanings that are available. Take the capacious word *Passion*, which has come to be used as a synonym for Jesus' suffering.[5] But passion means much more—including inspired, zealous commitment and desire. With this in mind, Jesus' death can be read in a more complex way. We can notice texts that are often ignored, like the observation in the Letter to the Hebrews (12:2) that Jesus goes to the cross "for the joy that was set before him." When he turns his face to Jerusalem, the Gospels suggest that he is caught up in a powerful, irresistible impulse that perhaps even he cannot explain—a passion. As he overturns the tables of the money-changers in the Temple, his disciples remember the verse "zeal [*zelos*] for your house will consume me" (John 2:17).

With agape blinders taken off, Jesus appears in the Gospel stories as a charismatic and threatening presence as well as a gentle and loving one. It is his miraculous powers and scandalous teachings that draw comment, not his self-denial. He seems to have given off a sense of electric power. Some of his relatives and friends think that he has gone mad—that he is "beside himself"—and set out to restrain him. To turn these accounts into a tale of gentle self-sacrificial love involves a lot of engineering and leaves us with a figure so morally exalted that he floats off into outer space, cutting us off not just from the texts, but from our own experiences of being loved and loving.

Supposedly timeless definitions are always rooted in the preoccupations of their time. The motif of self-sacrifice came to special prominence

---

5. From the Greek root, *path*. Chapter 1 of Acts says that "After his passion he presented himself alive to them." Many recent translations change that to "After his suffering . . ."

in the context of two world wars. It helped to give meaning to the tragic loss of life—and to evade it. A foreign visitor who witnessed the way the British do "Remembrance" told me he thought that the emotional trauma of the wars had never been fully processed. The poppies, crosses, and ceremony were a shortcut. Even today, the exaltation of heroic altruistic love threatens to push other forms of love into the shadows. In her study of older women in an Anglican church, Abby Day notices how their everyday acts of devotion—from polishing the pews to making the tea—are overlooked.[6] Cleaners and care workers remain at the bottom of society in esteem and reward in part because they do not fit a more masculine model of heroic self-sacrifice.

Love is many things. It can shake us up and set our hearts on fire, or be felt in dependable routines and considerate thoughtfulness. It can be gentle and considered or passionate and wild. It is known in small acts of kindness and extravagant gestures of altruism. We can see it in the pictures that the photographer Richard Billingham takes of his alcoholic family without hiding the difficulties of their situation.[7] Some passionate acts that on the surface seem imprudent and embarrassing, we know deep down to be magnificently right. The fact that we cannot define love does not mean that we do not know it when we see it, or come to recognize it later on, or that one kind is better than another.

It is ironic that love became a mainstream cultural theme in the 1960s just as many people were turning away from the churches. The revolution that unfolded under the banner "all you need is love" also marked the start of a rapid phase of decline in church attendance. Disciplinarians of all kinds were right to be horrified by the "summer of love," for what was being celebrated was a love that was outside anyone's control or special ownership. What might have been a meeting point for church and world turned out to be a parting of the ways.

It is perfectly possible to say that Christianity is about love, without making any special claim to it, or thinking that Christians have it all nailed down. Love is, in any case, not all you need. It is neither the engine of all human goodness and achievement, nor the only way to think about God, nor all that matters in life. In a memoir that is a chronicle of creativity in the midst of difficult relationships, the novelist Elizabeth Jane Howard draws a conclusion about "the extreme *importance* of truth, which, it seems to me

6. Day, *Religious Lives,* 75.

7. Billingham, *Ray's A Laugh.*

now, should be continually searched for and treasured when any piece of it is found."[8] That is not "the" answer either, but it reminds us that there are many points on a moral compass—and no one "true north."

8. Howard, *Slipstream*, 477. Italics original.

8. MY EXPERIENCE OF PRAYER

NPH

IT IS IMPOSSIBLE TO talk about experience of prayer without making a claim to have prayed. But such a claim cannot be made with any certainty: prayer is not the sort of thing I can claim to have done—or not done. Converging with this cautionary note is the fact that there are no experts in prayer. Articulateness on the subject does not indicate proficiency. This therefore can only be a process report, from within, with nothing definitive about it.

My personal story is one of becoming dissatisfied with a whole succession of forms of prayer which have come my way at various times. The list includes the rosary, various forms of eucharistic action, the monastic office, contemplative prayer, and corporate charismatic prayer. All of these in their day I took with great seriousness, but none have retained much purchase on my mind and imagination except the charismatic dimension, and that only as a loosener. This pattern of recurrent dissatisfaction could of course be put down to instability or even unfaithfulness, but I suspect that line of interpretation comes too easily.

It now seems that if the language of prayer means anything, I have been most prayerful when not consciously praying. I am thinking of times when I have felt most alive, most connected, most drawn into a spirit of praise, of gratitude, of pleading. Such occasions come unbidden, by surprise. They have nothing to do with prayer if that is understood as something I do. We are concerned here with the mystery of everything, not of a set-apart God who invites into a disembodied other world. Long ago there was discussion in the monastery as to whether it was acceptable to spend the time of personal prayer walking in the monastery garden. A colleague was of the opinion that it was, "provided you are not seduced by the sunset." I was puzzled: to be seduced by the sunset seemed to me an excellent thing. Would that it occurred more often! This anecdote illustrates two completely different understandings of what prayer is.

The trouble with all methods of prayer is that they presuppose certain images of God and patterns of behavior. They may be helpful triggers or catalysts for a time, but if held on to they constrict the spirit and prevent prayer. A monk once encouraged me: "It's no good thinking you can learn to pray by taking other people's prayers out of books." The forms, the methods are not themselves prayer, but their use can create the illusion that we are praying. More seriously, favorite words and methods can hold us in childish dependency and subservient behavior patterns. Piety and devotion can be enemies of faith.

The whole thing is a process of trial and error—like life, because it is life. Faith is about growing up—or not—and that is a process of trial and error. We engage in a variety of projects and relationships, trying out different identities, sometimes with tragic consequences. But such an outcome does not mean we should not have gone that way; it only means that particular venture represents a possibility that did not come off. It is vital, and has to do with prayer, that we continue to live in a world of possibilities. I have a sense of the various ways of prayer with which I have been involved. Each now seems a borrowed identity, an identity that did not quite fit and that therefore could not be sustained. But then that has been true of my life so far, or at least of a good deal of it: a succession of forms of life that I embraced but that turned out to be unsatisfying. Some commentators stress continuity in their remarks about prayer. I am much more conscious of discontinuity.

What about the nub of this, the present? There is no way back from the exposure and discomfort of what I have described. As far as I can see it is about unlearning bad images of God, not least that of the all-powerful and all-knowing one whose infinite resources are always available. God the arch-carer. That image is no more than a blown-up idealization of certain human qualities. This image of God is quite foreign to most people's experience, and certainly to mine. Even more importantly, it does bad things for our self-image, tending to restrain the creative spontaneity of which we are capable. It plays down the painful opportunity we have to take responsibility for our own lives.

I am commending prayer as a gift rather than a practice, a disturbing gift that can threaten our practice and suggest a change of life. There is much more prayer about, I suggest, than we are routinely aware of, if only we can be relaxed enough to tune in to it. For large parts of my life I have tried too hard to pray. The practice has too often been a distraction from the gift. The point is to recognize and stay with the gift. Not always easy, but rewarding.

What then of Jesus and the church? It is often said that we are given access by way of the Holy Spirit to Jesus' relationship with the Father, and that the Lord's Prayer offers a reliable direction for our prayer. There is a way of so exalting Jesus' relationship with the Father-God as to eviscerate both his human context and ours. There is also a way of so privileging the Father-image among all the possible images of God that it becomes definitive and therefore oppressive. If coupled with giving a central place to Jesus' prayer in Gethsemane this image tends to generate or at least confirm an overly passive frame of mind. It favors putting up with things rather than taking responsibility. The other side of the Gethsemane story is the injunction of Jesus to the sleepy disciples to "watch and pray." Religious people often allow the first verb to be overlaid by the second, but the text says we are to keep our eyes open. The priority is on continuing to look at and ponder on what is happening, without premature or a priori judgment.

As to the Lord's Prayer, the tendency among Christians to say that it is distinctive does not take its origins in the Jewish Scriptures seriously enough.[1] But even on the supposition that it was different from all that went before, and that Jesus exhorted his first followers to pray that way, it by no means follows that we are to attempt to do the same. Indeed, such a supposition cannot bear serious scrutiny. We cannot be certain what "this way" was for Jesus, or for his first followers. Even if we could have that certainty it would get us no further, for we are not they. Take, for instance, a phrase like "Your kingdom come." What immediate resonance does such a phrase have for us? Scholars of course inform us of layers of possible meaning, but that is the work of the historian, not of the theologian. In day-to-day terms the phrase remains cryptic and often opaque.

How can it be the case that Christians continue to use the Lord's Prayer? We should not overlook the role of traditional prayer forms as expressions of identity. It is likely that those who still use this form of words are doing their own thing with it. In any case I am arguing not so much against its continued use as against any assumption that it can of itself guide or direct our praying. The New Testament has Jesus saying, "The Spirit blows where it will," but the common insistence on the Spirit's special connection with established ways or current orthodoxies tends to anesthetize

1. See Parker, *Living Text*, chapter 4.

us to the world of wonder, beauty, and terror in which we find ourselves. True prayer is our reconnection with present reality and its possibilities.

9. HOW FORTUNE-TELLING TAUGHT ME TO PRAY

LW

As a child I absorbed the idea that prayer meant addressing God reverently with eyes closed, hands together. It was said to be hard, and it certainly felt it. A lapse made me anxious: if something bad happened to a loved one it might be my fault for not having prayed enough. Looking back, it seems that I was trying to placate an all-powerful Father who could never be satisfied. Today, in the wake of charismatic renewal and other changes in church life, this whole approach may seem antique. More enthusiastic and expressive kinds of prayer are on offer. Kneeling is out and outstretched arms and upturned heads are in. Online prayer is catching on, too. But what look like big changes from the outside don't feel like that from the inside, at least to me.

One thing that brought me back to prayer was studying what it meant in practice for different people. I found that prayers are not always addressed to "God" in a traditional sense but to some higher or benevolent power, human or divine (or both). There is huge variety. In a study of prayer slips left in a hospital chapel, the anthropologist Peter Collins found messages like these:

> A huge thanks to all those in A&E for saving my son's life.

> Altho I don't believe in a god, I think that jesus was a good person who can help others. So please can you make [name] better.

> Still miss you millions [name]. Lots of love [name].

> Dear God in heaven save my dad and I will be with you for evermore.[1]

---

1. Collins, "Analysis," 197, 204.

Visiting Manchester in May 2017, shortly after a suicide bomber had killed twenty-three people leaving a pop concert, I joined a large gathering in a city square where we paid our respects to the dead around a growing pile of cards, candles, flowers, balloons, and soft toys. There was silence, despite the large number gathered there. Tributes left on cards and other items said things like:

> All my love to those involved. You are in my prayers.

> Your angels are stars in the sky may they shine bright
> and guide us and protect.

> After a storm—the sun always shines and warms you—
> let there be love.[2]

One reason for praying is that it is something to do when you don't know what else to do. That may be an evasion or an act of great love: there are no guarantees. Often prayer involves placing concerns in a different frame of reference, bringing them into connection with something or someone good and holy. When prayer is a response to crisis and loss of control, it may mean putting things into the hands of loving ancestors, guardian angels, nurses and doctors, or God. It may involve a shift of attention and reference and a connection to something "higher," or the making of a ritual gesture that simply externalizes something. It may involve holding people and situations "in the light," as Quakers say, or "giving them back to the universe," as others put it.

Working on a research project that involved interviews with Muslim women in various European countries, I was struck by how some spoke of prayer as a place of escape and expansion, in societies where the spaces they could occupy were often very constrained. They gave the impression that prayer opened a rich world of interiority and connection. Trapped in tedious and stressful jobs in countries where they did not always feel at home, they found refuge and empowerment in moments of prayer throughout the course of the day. It was empowering, subversive, expansive. I realized that prayer is not necessarily a matter of will and discipline, but may involve letting go and opening up. That can be an act of faith, hope, or courage, since you do not know what, if anything, you will receive.

A further expansion in my understanding came, even more unexpectedly, through research with "fortune-tellers." Here in an often despised

---

2. All actual examples.

arena of "superstition," I found great insight. My research involved participation in spiritualist groups, and in one-to-one readings with mediums. I
spent evenings in people's homes when a psychic would be hired to give
readings to all of those invited, after which we reassembled around the
kitchen table for animated discussion about what had "come through,"
punctuated by laughter and a good dose of skepticism. It was largely but
not exclusively a women's world, and the appeal was obvious: how often
does anyone take a serious interest in you and your loved ones and offer
engaged reflections and guidance about your life?

Much that was said by the mediums was uncannily accurate, and
nearly all of it was helpful. I did not find the fatalism or credulity that is so
often associated with fortune-telling. "Can you take that?" mediums often
ask about a message or reading, and a refusal does not offend. It has more
to do with co-creation than passive reception. As the mysterious alchemist
Fludd says in Hilary Mantel's eponymous novel, "It is true that, in a way,
I can tell the future. But not in the way you think. I can make you a map.
I can indicate to you a choice of turnings. But I cannot travel the route on
your behalf."[3] Fortune-telling leaves room for doubt, interpretation, conversation, contestation, and choice.

The popular catch-all term "fortune-telling" is often rejected by prac-
titioners, who more often refer to themselves as psychics, mediums, sensi-
tives, and spiritualists. Some draw careful distinctions between the skills
and activities of psychic, medium, and fortune-teller/diviner, even though
in practice many use all these skills in a single "reading." Astrology and
tarot card reading are more obviously about divination, but these too may
be combined with one or more of the other activities. The seer or diviner is
found in all societies, in all times. To practice divination is to take practical steps to discern hidden meanings and guidance here in the midst of
our lives—in a flight of birds, the lines on a palm, the alignment of stars,
a pack of cards, communications with spirits of the dead. Fortune-telling
situates us in a framework of forces and powers. The point is to open one-
self to inspiration in order to discern more clearly what is going on and
when is the appropriate moment at which to act. The living and dead,
spirits and material objects, and a supreme being, may be invoked and
involved. Spirit-guides and sacred sites, scrying mirrors and tarot cards,
coffee grounds and tea leaves, assist in opening minds, amplifying weak
signals, and discerning the meaning of a situation.

3. Mantel, *Fludd*, 177.

Deep within my inner resistance to prayer had been a childhood understanding of it as a transaction with an all-powerful God before whom I felt both powerless and responsible. My experience of fortune-telling helped to exorcise that demon by introducing me to a very different cosmology. Here was neither a determined universe—governed by law, God, or fate—nor an entirely open one in which it is all up to us and I can "be anything I want to be." Instead, seers help people to become more sensitive to lives and situations, thereby opening up new potential. Like some kinds of prayer, fortune-telling can help when our normal ways of thinking and acting are failing. If you are stuck, the medium can draw awareness to more options. In situations where we have no clear sense of what a good outcome to a difficult situation might even be, prayer and divination offer means of creative discernment that generate possibilities.

Divination, dream interpretation, prophecy, and apocalyptic are all found in the Bible, often closely connected. Joseph has a silver cup that he uses as a divining instrument, and he wins Pharaoh's favor through marvelous dream interpretation. Gideon is possessed by a "spirit from the Lord" who "puts on" Gideon in a trance possession. Aaron carries the oracle stones "Urim" and "Thummim." The prophets dream dreams and see visions. Jesus' birth is foretold by angels, magi, and a star. Jesus himself speaks with the dead—Moses and Elijah—and foretells the future.

None of this has to be seen as either religious or superstitious. In Anthony Powell's series of novels *A Dance to the Music of Time* there is no God and no obvious moral order, but the narrative pivots around uncanny signs and meaningful coincidences. There is no question about the agency of Powell's characters, but they are playing out a destiny as well, whether or not they hear what he calls the "secret harmonies."

There is nothing wrong with accepting that we cannot know for certain whether prayer and divination are appropriate to the sort of universe we inhabit, for the evidence is ambiguous. In a recent survey, many people reported that they prayed "on the off chance something could change." That is also why people throw coins into holy wells and streams. You do not have to know for sure that it will have any effect: it may just be a hunch, a hypothesis, a cosmic lottery ticket. Prayer and divination, even when practiced by people who remain agnostic about their effectiveness, are often more than a self-interested bet. They are an implicit act of hope that things are not wholly disenchanted: that there is a heart in the heartless world and that we can help give it more of one. Calling this just a gamble is trivializing. Someone who prays for a friend with cancer is not necessarily reaching for the snake oil; prayer may come from a very different place in them.

The idea that the course of things is preordained by a fatherly God or, at the other extreme, utterly devoid of humanly significant meaning, is no more rational than belief in the kind of conditioned agency assumed by divination—indeed, theistic or atheistic determinism seems to strain the evidence more. Just saying a prayer without committing to its truth or falsity can tip people towards life. Whether someone is reading a horoscope or saying the Our Father, they may be opening themselves to deeper meanings and higher powers.

10. SPIRIT AND SACRAMENTS— NOTES ON A PERCEIVED DISJUNCTION

NPH

Like everybody else, I bowed my head
during the consecration of the bread and wine,
I lifted my eyes to the raised host and raised chalice,
I believed (whatever it means) that a change occurred.

I went to the altar rails and received the mystery
on my tongue, returned to my place, shut my eyes fast, made
an act of thanksgiving, opened my eyes and felt
time starting up again.
    There was never a scene
when I had it out with myself or with another.
The loss of faith occurred offstage. Yet I cannot
disrespect words like "thanksgiving" or "host"
or even "communion wafer." They have an undying
pallor and draw, like well water far down.[1]

AT THE AGE OF ninety, Sebastian Moore bravely and generously noted in his book *The Contagion of Jesus* his chronic boredom during the daily community mass in which as a monk of Downside he participated. It is important to stress that what is in play here is not simply what Harold MacMillan would have called "a little local difficulty." Something deeper and more universal is at stake. This unguarded admission from someone with a lifelong, reflective interest in and commitment to eucharistic

1. From Heaney, "Out of This World," 47.

practice seems to me a breath of fresh air. Moore tells the reader that he performs a particular mental gymnastic to remind himself of the significance of the sacramental act, but his need to do so reveals malfunctioning liturgy at the root of the boredom.

Reflecting on the difficulty of observing the custom of one minute's silence at big football matches in honor of a person or group who have died, Mihir Bose, the BBC's former chief sports correspondent, said that this practice is "in danger of becoming a mere ritual, that we go through."[2] The Second Vatican Council, in seeming contrast to this notion of a "mere ritual," affirmed as beyond argument that the liturgy is "the source and summit of the whole life of the Church" (*Constitution on the Liturgy*). This extraordinary claim dramatically mistakes sign for reality, thus inviting us to dwell in a parallel universe constituted by liturgical actions. The background to Bose's remark is the frequent tendency of football crowds, or sections of the crowd, to disrupt the silence in a disrespectful manner, suggesting that the ritual has lost whatever power it once had. It has become a contrivance rather than a living act. The Council's claim does not allow such a possibility, but rather seems to embody it, in its implication that liturgy is somehow superior to life. My suggestion is that as sacraments are signs of life, this is a blind alley.

In essence a sacrament is a spontaneous response, otherwise it is at best nothing, at worst some form of psychic invasion. Thus a minute's silence demanded of a football crowd is undoubtedly a psychic invasion for some, who are simply not equipped or not ready to play their allotted part in a ritual from which they feel alien or to which they are hostile. It can be the same for many participants in more obviously religious events, where what is happening neither emerges from nor speaks to their condition. To blame hooliganism or unbelief is to miss the point. Something corporate and systemic is in play. There is a parallel here with the clerical sex abuse crisis, where merely deploring the moral delinquency of individual priests and religious fails to confront the factors in our ecclesiastical culture that facilitate not only such abuse but also its concealment.

At the end of a liturgy to celebrate a marriage the presiding priest told the congregation that this, the church service, was the most important part compared to the all-night party that was to follow. This seemed to me to exemplify a divorced sacramentalism in which the claim that only the sign controlled by the church is sacred trivializes the other to the detriment of

2. Bose, Mihir, BBC Radio 4, February 10, 2008.

both. In this instance at least, the party was no less part of the sacrament than the church service that preceded it, for it manifested the link with the life of this couple and the circle of life surrounding and supporting them.

Sacramental practice, or as it is sometimes called "the sacramental life," has become seriously and often dangerously disconnected from the life of which the sacraments claim to be signs. From this point of view the current revival of eucharistic processions and adoration is a countersign. These practices teeter on the edge of claiming that where the consecrated host is there is Jesus, with the implication that whatever else may be happening cannot affect the meaning of the sign itself. Here the language of "real presence," fruit of ancient, unresolved conflict in the church, is unhelpful. The late mediaeval feast of Corpus Christi makes the point aggressively in saying to Cathars, Lollards, and other such heretics, "Look, here we have the real thing." The same state of mind is evident in the Roman Catholic tendency to have "mass with everything," as if only in a prescribed liturgy, and that of the Eucharist in particular, can we be sure of the Spirit's presence. The dead end of this brand of theology can be found as early as Aquinas's answer to the question whether, if a priest in saying the words of consecration intends to consecrate all the bread in the marketplace, it would be consecrated. His answer is yes, thus demonstrating a remarkable degree of commitment to the notion of the validity of the sacramental words at the cost of all seriousness. What the purpose would be of such an act of consecration is not faced.

In an appendix to his book *I Believe in the Holy Spirit*, Yves Congar reflected on the fact that in the modern Catholic Church "three white things," the pope, the Eucharist, and the Virgin, occupy center stage.[3] While in no sense hostile to any of these three, Congar surmises that their overwhelming predominance results from the undeveloped state of the doctrine of the Holy Spirit in the Western church. Our present sacramental practice militates against sensitivity to the voice of the Spirit. It is still, in theory at least, a mortal sin for a Roman Catholic not to attend mass on a Sunday or holiday of obligation. There is no comparable stricture, indeed no stricture at all, on any failure to heed and follow the Spirit's prompting.

The idea of regular sacramental observance as being the sure means of access to divine life runs deep in the Catholic psyche. Two moments from the New Testament might serve as counter-instances to a tradition that exaggerates and so in the end impoverishes the role of sacraments.

---

3. Congar, *I Believe in the Holy Spirit*, vol. III, Appendix.

John the Baptist predicted that the one who would come after him would baptize "with the Holy Spirit and with fire," a scary image of an uncontrollable transformation scene. When I asked a priest why in view of this text we still persist in water baptism he thought I was proposing another sacrament, and replied that busy parish priests did not have time to think about things like that. Even Catholic charismatic renewal, which at its best has the great merit of seriously invoking and waiting upon the Spirit, fell into the same trap in its schedule for the "Life in the Spirit Seminars," which placed something called "Baptism in the Spirit" in the sixth week of the course. In this way it succeeded in manufacturing only another sacrament. The other New Testament moment is the story in the Acts of the Apostles of Peter and Cornelius, when Peter recognizes that Cornelius and his household have already received the Holy Spirit without being formally baptized. The story provides evidence of an uneasiness already in the early church about the place of the sacraments within the Christian life. Such uneasiness could be helpful, but of no use here is the historic divide between "Protestant" and "Catholic" theologies of the sacraments, since neither addresses these concerns.

A counter-argument would be that as Jesus instituted the sacraments we should surely beware of underplaying them. How well I remember the labored and tortuous efforts of our professors of theology to convince us that Jesus did so. The medievals settled on seven sacraments, but the number is arbitrary in the sense that it could easily have been more—or less. Luther reduced authorized sacraments to two, the authentically biblical ones as he understood the matter: baptism and Eucharist. Today, no attempt to link Christian rites or offices in any straightforward way to the mind of Jesus can survive critical scrutiny.

For theology in the high Middle Ages to think was to systematize. Sacraments did not escape this tendency, with the unfortunate though not strictly necessary consequence that they came to be thought of as a system. Nowadays this is a subplot of the modern habit of referring to "the Catholic belief system," a usage doubtfully compatible with a living faith. I used to enjoy saying to the largely Protestant student body at Queen's Theological College in Birmingham that I wanted lots more sacraments, a mere seven being hopelessly inadequate to point up the multifarious wonders and delights of our universe. Sacraments are no more and no less than signs of the transforming Spirit who cannot be boxed in by the carefully laid plans of liturgists.

A friend's question is apposite: "If the pope, the Eucharist and the Virgin cease to have such a dominant position in our approach to religion, what should we then do to become attuned to the working of the Spirit?" This question arises in part from the mistaken assumption that it is all about what we do. The deeper answer is that there is no answer other than that we find out in living, by trial and error. No sacramental system can shield us from the hazards of this search. Teilhard de Chardin wrote: "I have not ceased to explore the dangers to which a man is subject when, forsaking the paths of traditional discipline, now for him sub-human, he seeks a road to heaven on which matter and flesh can pass into the birth of spirit."[4]

The artist and poet David Jones reminds us in his poem "The Anathemata" that the priest guards the sacred sign "more precariously than he knows." Two examples follow of ways in which things can go badly awry. The first is James O'Toole's account of some dubious political uses to which sacramental and in particular eucharistic practice has been put in the USA: the forty hours' devotion as a weapon against "atheistic communism," and in the Second World War, going to frequent, regular confession and communion as a key part of the war effort.[5]

A second example is the custom of using the Eucharist to patrol the boundaries of the church.[6] We hedge the Eucharist about with rules as to who may receive and who may not. There is even a movement afoot to ensure that those not entitled to receive are informed of these restrictions. Since the ruling mindset in these matters stems from the Vatican, this approach demonstrates how the pope and the sacraments can form a toxic combination, to the detriment of the Spirit. These regulations are partly targeted at members of other churches and religions, but they have very much in mind Catholics judged in some way or other morally unsuitable to receive. If they could be strictly enforced no Catholic eucharistic congregations could long survive, given the range of allegedly disqualifying factors: cohabiting couples, gay couples, couples in canonically irregular marital situations, those using contraceptive devices, those who have not been to confession since last culpably missing mass, etc. The list is almost endless. It is true that these restrictions are widely ignored or not noticed, but that too is unhealthy in that it reflects a disconnection between the mind of the leadership and common practice.

4. Quoted by Raven, *Teilhard de Chardin*, 63.

5. O'Toole, ed., *Habits of Devotion*.

6. I owe this incisive phrase to the Anglican priest-ecumenist John Muddiman.

Finally, a significant moment of remembering. At the Easter vigil in a monastic church long ago the consecrated eucharistic hosts ran out, to the grave embarrassment of those presiding. In starkest contrast, one of the brethren used the incident to express the predicament of a monastic community that had given its allegiance to "the truth locked up in a cupboard and held onto in blind faith." No church, however large and venerable, has anywhere to go when the hosts run out and the cupboard is shown to be bare.

11. THE DANGEROUSLY UNNOTICED AMBIVALENCE OF THE CROSS

NPH

Licking their wounds
And flashing them around like decorations.
I hate it, I always hated it, and I am
A part of it myself.[1]

CHRISTIANS TEND TO SAY that salvation is to be found in the suffering of the crucified Jesus. I find myself wondering about the uses to which this claim is put, in the light of Heaney's remark. The sufferings of Jesus were, after all, particular: to wear them as a badge of identity is at least as likely to alienate as to reconcile.

Some will claim that this is the inescapable scandal of the cross: that which is for the good of all is not perceived by all to be so. But in our world of many faiths and none what frame of reference could establish such a claim? How could it be shown that this suffering alone is absolutely distinctive, is indeed defining of and transforming of all pain everywhere at all times? It can be argued that the sufferings of Jesus are intelligible only as an epitome of the suffering destiny of his people, Israel, whose sufferings are distinctive because of this people's chosenness. But to invoke this corporate dimension takes our present question no further. Why should other people, and peoples, take seriously the claim that this people's sufferings are distinctively salvific for all?

The French anthropologist René Girard popularized the idea that scapegoating has a crucial place in human affairs. This theory applied to Jesus becomes the claim that he is the willing scapegoat who, alone of all

---

1. Heaney, *Cure at Troy*, 2.

scapegoats, is then empowered to return in forgiveness of the scapegoaters. Discussions about the conscious intention of Jesus are endless, and endlessly inconclusive. My point is the more modest one that all images of powerlessness and self-emptying are ambivalent, and that this characteristic is dangerously unnoticed by their promoters. This chapter is a cautionary note addressed to uncritical use of the symbol of the crucified as our badge of identity.

Charles Wesley's hymn "Lo, He Comes with Clouds Descending," still commonly sung in churches in Advent, exalts the "glorious scars" of Jesus. Those Jews who rejected him when they had the chance to do otherwise are presented as "deeply wailing" when confronted with the glory of these scars. This text is at least to our ears antisemitic, but the point here is that Jesus' scars are used as the symbol of victory. Many more restrained Christian texts make similar use of Jesus' suffering. It is one thing to say "By his stripes we are healed," and mean by that a particular group of people. It is quite another to mean in principle everybody except those who reject the claim.

Francis of Assisi is often pictured as a reconciling, peacemaking person in the modern sense, with the stigmata confirming the claim. But the chronicler tells otherwise. When he tried to deter the sultan from continuing the war against the Crusaders, Francis first sought to convert him and then, failing that, to be martyred by him. Instead of playing Francis's game the sultan courteously provided him with an escort back to the Crusaders' camp. Notice how psychological and physical violence are both in play in Francis's version of Christian allegiance; the first in the attempt to convert, the second in the attempt to be martyred. The Crusaders fought under the sign of the cross, but so it would seem did Francis, who was in no doubt where lay the victory. His frustration was that the sultan would not play his part, whether as convert or as executioner. This is quite a different universe of discourse from modern notions of peacemaking.

An obvious move at this stage of the discussion is to say that Charles Wesley and Francis are both distorting the pristine message of the cross, which most modern Christians see as unambiguously reconciliatory. But where is this pristine message to be found? Consider, for instance, the fourth Gospel and the book of Revelation. The former has Jesus saying, "I, when I am lifted up from the earth, will draw all men to myself" (John 12:32). That is an image of power. Revelation then offers the superficially harmless image of the lamb who was slain, the utterly vulnerable creature easily destroyed by this-worldly powers. But this lamb is different: worthy of honor and power. Taken along with the thrashing of the dragon's tail as an image of the death-throes of a seemingly mighty empire, this language is profoundly subversive. Despite appearances the persecutor's power is waning, whereas we, this tiny group of obscure and persecuted people, have the real force with us. The implicit message is victory rather than reconciliation in the modern sense. The symbol of this victory is the slain lamb, the crucified Jesus.

On his visit to Ukraine, Pope John Paul II voiced to other Christian leaders his longing for unity. But at his first mass at Kyiv he said, "Land of Ukraine, drenched with the blood of martyrs, thank you for the example of fidelity to the Gospel, which you have given to Christians the world over."[2] Am I alone in finding the verb "drenched" chilling in this context? Whose blood? And at whose hands? The pope here taps into the ancient belief that the blood of the martyrs is the seed of the church, and that martyrdom is the highest form of Christian witness. But in the extremely complex religious geography of Ukraine these words could hardly be considered reconciliatory, and perhaps were not meant to be so. The implication is that victory lies with the martyrs, who in their turn have the closest possible affinity with the broken body and spilt blood of Jesus.

This, it could be argued, is exactly what Seamus Heaney is objecting to, reflecting of course on the Northern Irish situation. In her book *The Catholics of Ulster*, Marianne Elliot points out that both Nationalists and Unionists have interiorized a sense of suffering victimhood, and that this derives in each case from Christian symbols.[3] In his play *The Singer*, the Nationalist leader Pádraig Pearse affirmed the nexus between his own political aspiration and the story of Jesus: "One man can free a people as one Man redeemed the world."[4] There is a comparable sense of defensive/aggressive victimhood in the beleaguered identity of modern Unionism. The interesting thing for our purposes is that both Catholics and Protestants in the North owe allegiance to the symbol of the crucified. This symbol, far from resolving the conflict by transcending division, is itself part of the problem. It has proved fatally easy for each group to use it to buttress its own identity, each tending to identify its own pain, but not its enemy's, with that of Jesus. This is an example of a wider phenomenon:

2. John Paul II, *Pastoral Visit to Ukraine 2001*.

3. Elliot, *Catholics of Ulster*.

4. Pearse, *Singer*, 43

one of the forms of identity politically available in our world is that of the abused victim. In this climate the claim to have been abused is a claim to power, which in its turn is easily misused.

Each identity is an embattled one, envisaging its own victory. The relative disregard for human life that obtained over so many years in the North connects in part with notions of blood-sacrifice that also tap into versions of Christian faith. It is not enough merely to declare such images aberrant from the viewpoint of some imagined pure essence of Christianity. The inadequacy of this response was writ large at the time of the hunger strikes in the Maze prison, particularly in the days when a succession of coffins emerged from the prison. These coffins had a clear message: "We, the right-minded ones, appear helpless now, but our day is coming, and then it will go hard with you." Elliott notes that the discomfort and helplessness of constitutional Nationalists were palpable in the face of this phenomenon. Nor could the broadcast words of Margaret Thatcher—"A crime is a crime is a crime!"—touch the non-rational power of this symbol, rehearsing as it did the sacrificial violence characteristic of the Nationalist canon of history. The taunt of "betraying the patriot dead" was still potent against those Nationalists who sought another way.

This theme can be extended further by reflection on a belief as old as recorded history, and strong in eighteenth-century Britain, that the corpses of criminals have mystical properties.[5] The blood was especially, though not exclusively, prized, even to the extent of seeking to drink it from a newly decapitated body. This puts both the Christian story and that of the hunger strikers (whose funerals were attended by vast crowds) in a rather different perspective. Remember that what we continue to proclaim in the Eucharist is the death of Jesus "until he comes," that coming offering a hint of a world turned upside down, as in Bob Dylan: "The loser now will be later to win."[6] While the eucharistic theme needs much more work, it can already be said that none of the images in play are as unreservedly and unequivocally benign as modern "justice and peace" Christians might like to think.

5. Hibbert, *Roots of Evil*, 294–96.
6. Dylan, "Times They Are A'Changin.'"

12. JESUS WITHOUT EXAGGERATION I

NPH

TWELVE YEARS IN THE most multiracial, and therefore most multifaith, district of Britain—Handsworth in Birmingham—seems to have cured me of that habit of mind that took it for granted that Christian belief was superior to all others. This debate is usually conducted by Christians around claims for the uniqueness of Jesus, but uniqueness functions here as a codeword for superiority. Uniqueness as such is hardly problematic, as every person is unique, but contemporary Christians tend to think of other faiths rather in the way the Second Vatican Council thought of Christian bodies other than the Roman Catholic Church: they have elements of truth and sanctification, but they lack the fullness that is given only to us.

It is precisely this claim to a definitive fullness of truth and life that left me in the course of my Handsworth years. It is the claim attributed to Jesus himself by the most high-toned of the canonical Gospels, the fourth, which has him saying "I am the way, and the truth, and the life" (John 14:6). This saying would not be problematic if it meant something like, "I'm onto something very big, I'm very much alive, and I'm going right through with it, whatever the odds, because nothing else matters." That is a state of mind that many people have been in at one time or another, though it often gets repressed. But the claim helped to launch Christianity on a much more ambitious trajectory: "There is no other name under heaven given among men by which we must be saved" (Acts 4:12). Most modern Christians do not take this literally, but they hang on to the note of superiority.

I am not claiming to have thought my way out of this assumption about Jesus. It is rather that it has left me, a change that happened so gradually as to be almost imperceptible. In Handsworth I lived surrounded by Sikhs, Hindus, Muslims, and others, while never having an extended conversation with any of my neighbors about religion. It came to seem somehow absurd to suppose that all these people lacked something that only Jesus could provide. Their lives were not shapeless or indeterminate. Many of their beliefs and practices seemed not so different in kind from ours, once I had allowed my sense of their seeming strangeness to be succeeded by a reflection on the comparable strangeness that Christian beliefs and practices must present to those not already convinced. Considering Christianity in relation to other religious and philosophical traditions, a friend wrote recently: "It goes further, is more unbelievable than the world's great wisdoms, but not against them." I no longer understand how it is possible to be thus categorical in the assertion of Christianity's superiority.

Can this change really be accounted for by prolonged exposure to a multifaith environment? No. What this environment did was to erode the last vestiges of a waning state of mind. When challenged by the close proximity and observation of people of other faiths my vestigial sense of Christianity's superiority could not be sustained. The multifaith environment showed me this, confirming a question already in my mind. It seems impossible to trace the origins of this change. Perhaps I never really believed in the superiority claimed for Jesus, but accepted it because I knew nothing else, or had no reason to question it. In my childhood it was an element in that taken-for-granted religious superstructure that I learned by heart. Current theology has pressed the point further, with its stress on the overwhelming centrality of christology and a lifeless trinitarianism. But once the claim to superiority is abandoned, is Christianity deprived of its substance? Can a version of Christian faith that does not depend upon this claim satisfy the requirements of coherence and authenticity? And if Jesus is not "the way, the truth and the life," who or what is he? Are there acceptable versions of his story which are not triumphalist or totalitarian in the sense that I am now constrained to reject? Theology has not yet, I think, seriously addressed these questions.

It comes to me as I write that to make Jesus everything is perhaps in the end to reduce him to nothing. If all particularity is lost in his cosmic exaltation what is left of him? This may in part explain how he has come to mean so many different and often contradictory things. Once his particularity is lost sight of, he becomes a kind of sanctified space into which people project their hopes and fears. Perhaps this process started early. It was in any case far advanced by the time Christian thinkers began to speak of the union of the human and divine in him. Has that way of seeking to unite in a single person an idea of divinity with an idea of humanity gone so far away from any recognizable human person as to be void of meaning? Is the formula "true God and true man" anything more than a convenient abstraction, theoretically reconciling different versions of Jesus but in practice saying nothing of substance about him?

This Jesus is constituted by things we are supposed to know about in other ways. He partakes in something called the divine nature, as well as sharing with us our human nature. What is strange about him is not these entities but their combination in a single person. On this supposition we know what it is to be God, and we know what it is to be human. We do not know, except in Jesus, what it is to be both. If this is an attempt to secure his absolute difference from and superiority to everyone else it succeeds, I suggest, only in making Jesus strange in the non-mysterious sense of the word. He is odd, even quaint, an awkward and unconvincing composite rather than a living person.

There was enthusiasm, at the time, for the exhibition of Christian art "Seeing Salvation" at the National Gallery.[1] Its focus was the portrayal over the centuries and in different cultures of very diverse versions of Jesus. From one point of view this variety is a sign of vitality in the tradition, an indication of Jesus' capacity to be all things to all people. Such diversity could be seen as confirming the claims traditionally made for him. Another viewpoint would rather suggest that what is happening in all these portrayals is an idealization of the human in terms acceptable within each period and culture. This suggestion is not that there is deceit or manipulation of the evidence, but rather an unconscious process of projection. These portrayals say nothing about Jesus but a great deal about each culture's ideal.

What must in any case be said is that we have not the slightest idea of what Jesus looked like. If he can be imaged in such a variety of ways, does it make sense to suppose that these portrayals have anything to do with him? Again the question comes: if he is everything, can he be anything? Maybe I'm beginning to feel something of what Borges said about Shakespeare, whom he pictured as a person of no substance in himself but capable of identifying with every imaginable human state.

---

1. The images are reproduced in Finaldi, *The Image of Christ.*

13. JESUS WITHOUT EXAGGERATION II

LW

> Blessed assurance, Jesus is mine;
> Oh, what a foretaste of glory divine!
> Heir of salvation, purchase of God,
> Born of the Spirit, washed in his blood . . .[1]

IT IS NOT ONLY Jews and Muslims who think that Christians exaggerate Jesus; plenty of Christians think so too. I have spoken to churchgoers in several countries who admit that Jesus does not mean that much to them: like the evangelical in a US megachurch who said with a mixture of ruefulness and relief that he left Jesus to his wife who "spends a lot more time with him than me," or the lady in northern England who walked out of chapel one day saying to herself "blessed assurance, Jesus doesn't have to be mine anymore," and never went back.

Whether it is Jesus' divinity or humanity that is being overplayed, it is the attempt to produce something too simple and definitive that results in something artificial. As a short-lived and unhappy member of the Third Wellington Methodist Brownies, I remember being taken to an evangelical chapel service for the first time. The sermon was all about Jesus and the text was "I am the way, the truth, and the life." The preacher told us that all we had to do was accept this and we would be saved. I felt shocked and cheated. Why hadn't I been told this before! I might have been damned for want of clearer instructions. But soon the doubt set in. Surely there must be more to being Christian than that. The fact that I can recall this incident so clearly suggests a child's sensitivity to the attempt to boss, confine, and intimidate.

---

1. "Blessed Assurance." Popular Christian hymn, lyrics by Fanny Crosby, 1873.

I have spoken to many Christians who feel that they ought to believe that Jesus is all-important, is God, but cannot. This is easy to understand if God has been presented as the Almighty all-everything. The bigger and more transcendent God becomes, the more of an omni-God, the harder to make sense of an incarnation as a human being—it befuddles the mind. If Jesus is himself superhuman, he ceases to be human at all.

Docetism is the name of the heresy that tried to square this circle by saying that Jesus only appeared to be human but was really a god who descended briefly to earth. But Christians are routinely docetic whenever they talk about Jesus as if he were utterly unlike the rest of us. When his birth is miraculous, his life sinless, his suffering unparalleled, and his death and resurrection utterly unique, he loses connection with the rest of us. This is the Jesus who patiently puts up with the human condition and dutifully plays his part in the knowledge that it will all come out right in the end, following a foreordained plan. What's human about that? As the poet Stevie Smith exclaims in exasperation:

> Oh Christianity, Christianity
> Why do you not answer our difficulties?
> If he was God He was not like us,
> He could not lose.[2]

The opposite swing of the pendulum is to "demythologize" Jesus so much that he becomes human-all-too-human. This leads to exaggeration too. Some historical reconstructions, like Géza Vermes's *Jesus the Jew*, make Jesus seem so similar to other Jewish teachers of his time that it is hard to imagine why his life could be of special interest. Monty Python's film *Life of Brian* played up this approach, deriving its humor from the idea of an ordinary Galilean being mistaken for the Christ: "he's not the Messiah, he's a very naughty boy." A wave of scholarly reconstructions culminated in the work of the "Jesus Seminar" in which scores of scholars and laymen voted on the historicity of the deeds and sayings of Jesus using criteria agreed on in advance. But the books that emerged, like John Dominic Crossan's *Jesus: A Revolutionary Biography*, make Jesus so acceptable that he does not hold our attention. Exaggerating Jesus' humanity results in a figure as lifeless as the one that is produced by exaggerating his divinity, it is just exaggeration in a different direction.

2. Smith, "Oh Christianity," 46.

Albert Schweitzer criticized an earlier crop of historical reconstructions of Jesus for trying to capture him with the historical method and serve up the result as the basis for a renewed Christian faith. Although there is much that the historian can teach us, Schweitzer thought that Jesus could only be known in life lived. As he put it in a much-quoted passage at the end of *The Quest of the Historical Jesus*:

> [Jesus] comes to us as One unknown, without a name, as of old, by the lakeside, He came to those men who knew Him not. He speaks to us the same words: "Follow thou me!" and sets us to the tasks which He has to fulfill for our time. He commands. And to those who obey Him, whether they be wise or simple, He will reveal himself in the toils, the conflicts, the sufferings which they shall pass through in His fellowship, and, as an ineffable mystery, they shall learn in their own experience Who He is.[3]

It is a lovely passage, but a bit exaggerated. Not all Christians have an experience of Jesus, let alone one like this, and even those people who do, don't necessarily become Christian.

A case in point. The novelist Rosamund Lehmann recounts a revelatory experience one day as she lay dozing. She felt herself flung to the ground and saw a figure with the "face of a real person, though not one I had ever seen before."[4] His beard is "short and crisp," his features pronounced but delicate, his eyes bright as stars. He leans towards her, gently encouraging her to rise. On waking, Lehman knows that she has encountered a great spiritual figure—but her overriding feeling is one of disappointment that it was not her beloved late daughter. Although Lehmann was later certain that she had "quite simply . . . encountered Jesus in the Garden of Gethsemane," she remained more interested in spiritualism than the church.[5]

The freshest accounts of Jesus rarely fit neatly with any particular theology. Akwaeke Emezi's novel *Freshwater* tells the story of Ada, the child of a Nigerian Catholic and a Malaysian, through the voices of the many gods, spirits, and demons who struggle to possess her. As a child, Ada adores Jesus, "which is exactly how he likes it . . . But he was never there for her . . . He couldn't even be bothered to materialize when she was just a little girl, when she really, really needed him. How can you leave

---

3. Schweitzer, *Quest*, 401.

4. Lehmann, *Swan in the Evening*, 135.

5. Lehmann, *Swan in the Evening*, 136–37.

a child alone like that?"[6] As Ada grows up, Jesus torments her: he makes her guilty, he makes her furious. Although she tries to banish "the fucking resurrected bastard"[7] he still appears sporadically, wearing her down with his loving smile. At the end of the novel, Ada makes peace with Jesus and with herself, finding a way to integrate him more harmoniously with her other spirits and demons.

I take from this the insight that there is no need to elevate Jesus so much that he shoots off into space or to tie him down so much that he loses his mysterious power. There is an in-between world where gods and spirits come within reach.

Some people hold apparently contradictory spiritual beliefs not because they are illogical, but because they are empirical and they trust their own awareness. I once shared a train journey with a security guard who, thanks to his Filipino wife, belonged to a house church in Lancashire that he loved very much. He was on his way back from a pilgrimage to the Holy Land and said that it had brought him closer to Jesus. He had been able to travel because a healer had released him from a chronic illness that his doctors could not treat. She told him that he was cursed by his sister-in-law and that the cure was to hold a live bullet in his palm for twenty-four hours: not easy, but he did it. At weekends he provided security for ghost tours in a medieval castle. He was sure the ghosts were real not only because he saw them, but because he carried out historical research in the library and found details that tallied with what he had seen. I asked him if he had ever had a similar supernatural encounter with Jesus and he said that he hadn't. He was not exaggerating one part of his experience so that the other bits fell away, nor cutting the cloth of experience to fit some idea of theological orthodoxy.

The sources of our knowledge about Jesus are diverse, contradictory, and provocative. The cracks in the written record are huge, unbridgeable, and lifegiving. They help to make things fluid, adaptable, and mysterious—like Jesus himself. The nineteenth-century mystical theologian Anna Kingsford helpfully suggests that we think of revelation as "reveilation"— not an illumination but a re-veiling. She describes it as a landscape whose "mountains and forests are suffused with soft and delicate mist, which half conceals and half discloses their shapes and tints. Even words, even pictures are symbols and veils."[8]

---

6. Emezi, *Freshwater,* 83.

7. Emezi, *Freshwater,* 86.

8. Kingsford, *Clothed with the Sun,* 18.

Those who say that their version of Jesus is the only one, or the only orthodox one, are exaggerating. To dismiss any other approach as relativism is to miss the point. No one invents their own Jesus from scratch: all of us, including Paul and the Gospel writers, start from somewhere in a pre-existent Jesus tradition. We can be critical about different accounts of Jesus without pretending that there is a timeless theological standpoint from which we start in making those criticisms. The sheer variety of christologies is more theologically interesting than the attempt to find an artificial coherence.

14. A SIN-CENTERED THEOLOGY AND ITS CONSEQUENCES

NPH

THE MEDIEVALS ASKED THE question of whether, but for sin, the savior of the world would have come. Scotus said yes, but Aquinas said no. As the latter's view prevailed in the church at large we are left with a sin-centered theology, which has destructive consequences. In Western theology the centrality of sin is reinforced by the phrase "original sin." Of course this does not mean that sin is the absolutely originating factor for us, but at least for the unwary it tends to push the theological narrative in that direction. Matthew Fox's *Original Blessing* incurred some ridicule but proposed a vital corrective.

In my ethics tutoring days I wearied of ordinands' essays which said that while in an ideal world such-and-such would be the case (how did they know? I wondered), in this fallen world it is not so. This makes sin so definitive that the entire human adventure is seen as against the odds, with God's main function being to jack the whole thing up from time to time. Aquinas, lacking our sense of history and knowing nothing of evolution, saw God as starting the creation off, humans promptly messing it up, and God having therefore to take special measures from time to time as and when things went wrong again—first with Moses and then with Jesus—to bring us up to scratch. This is a truly dismal version of the story so far, contrasting dramatically with Louis Armstrong's passionately felt "It's a wonderful world," or Jesus' "I am come that they might have life, and have it more abundantly." This sense of abundant life and wonder overriding all other considerations is key.

Aquinas did not originate the sin-centeredness of our theology, which picks up a human tendency to fear our creativity and the responsibility it entails. Paul's urgent hope that he might "by all means save some" strongly implies that very many would not be saved. Augustine's "massa damnata" echoes and reinforces this. Both these foundational figures clearly emphasized the power and range of sin, and assumed that those who did not follow their way were going to hell in a handcart. Susannah Wesley's image of her beloved son John as "a brand plucked from the burning" resonates far beyond the setting of a burning rectory from which the child was dramatically rescued. This thinking persists, limiting the scope of our sense of wonder, praise, and gratitude, teaching us to resist the persistent invitation to proceed further.

The medieval hymn known as the Exultet, still sung in Catholic churches at the Easter Vigil, finds in the phrase "O happy fault" its own way round this difficulty. Confronted with this, a priest theologian of my acquaintance replied, "That's only poetry." Matthew Fox's critics stressed the inadequacies of his book in a spirit that distracted from his insight. Bonhoeffer, arguing more subtly than Fox, said that if Christian ethics, in contrast to any other ethics, is our concern it begins with the unlearning of the knowledge of good and evil, or of right and wrong, a knowledge that springs from a divided consciousness. There is also Dame Julian of Norwich: "In our own eyes we cannot stand, in God's eyes we cannot fall. Both have truth, but God's insight is the deeper."[1] The point at issue in all these sources is that what is defining of us is gift and blessing, not sin.

Long ago my professor of dogmatic theology put the question: could God have created a world without evil? This professor replied morosely that he supposed God could have done so. I knew something was going wrong here, but could not see my way beyond this remarkably downbeat utterance. A sixteen-year-old boy of my acquaintance was bewildered by the question. "Surely," he said, "that is exactly what God is doing!" He saw this world as the best of all possible worlds in the making. What else can it be if we take seriously the idea of it as God's creation? A sin-centered theology cannot appropriate this conviction.

Classical Christian theology saw in Jesus a decisive step in the human project. In whatever way we contemporary Christians may choose to interpret this story, we cannot settle for Jesus being no more than one who gets us out of our latest mess. This is far too unambitious a starting point. Instead of the picture of Jesus as parachuted into our desperate situation as a divine rescue act, what about the possibility that the situation produced him? Since this is true of all humans, and we insist he is human, why should

1. Julian of Norwich, *Revelation of Love,* 131.

this not be the case? The suggestion is that a point has been reached in human development that led to what we might call the Jesus project of taking the story a decisive step further. There is a strongly evolutionary note here which refuses to allow sin a defining role.

In *Let This Mind Be In You: The Quest for Identity from Oedipus to Christ*, Sebastian Moore develops a new understanding of the traditional Christian teaching on original sin. It is, he suggests, the voice of original sin, not the doctrine, which puts sin at the center. This is the voice which whispers insistently that we are no good. Yet in the so-called Penny Catechism of my religious childhood that voice is dominant, seeking to interiorize a negative self-image: "Our natural inclinations are prone to evil from our very childhood, and if not corrected by self-denial they will certainly carry us to hell."[2] Unimaginable harm has been done, and continues to be done, by this voice. Moore sees original sin as a state of arrested development, an inertial resistance to growing out of the first stage of human consciousness. It entails a flight from understanding, a refusal of the gifted creativity that at root we are, and are destined to become more fully. A sin-centered theology distorts everything, not least the sense of sin itself, which cannot be taken seriously.

It is noteworthy that John Mahoney's book *The Making of Moral Theology* does not begin in earnest with the Bible or the Fathers, but with the practice of personal confession. In the theory and practice of that sacrament, and most notably in the development of the penitentials, we trace the entrenchment of an explicitly sin-centered moral theology. This same attitude still obtains in the deplorable insistence within the Catholic Church on confession before first communion, an outlandish practice to propose to a child. Meanwhile, by a supreme irony, adult Catholics have largely outgrown the practice, though not necessarily the theology.

Here is a story against myself. Newly ordained, inexperienced, and caught by surprise, I was suddenly asked to hear a confession. I did not know the penitent, who was only an anxious voice through the grille. "I have had sexual intercourse with my boyfriend," she blurted out. From somewhere deep in myself, out of reach of my liberal outlook at the time, came the words "Don't let it happen again!" My response to the unfortunate penitent is a copybook example of an act-centered moral theology.

Moves away from this approach, as from a law-based morality, are of course to be welcomed. Karl Rahner propounded the notion of a

---

2. Catholic Church, *Penny Catechism*, 344.

fundamental option: what counts in a person's life is the underlying direction rather than particular behaviors. But the fundamental option remains a choice between good and evil. This idealizes the human condition by leaving out the place of learning, as Marshall McLuhan saw in pointing out that the hand that does not erase cannot write the true word. Meanwhile the fashion for virtue ethics seems to take for granted that we already have adequate knowledge of what constitutes a life of virtue. Yet this, it seems to me, can only be discerned in living, which means by trial and error.

Questions of identity arise here. Someone who behaves in an unforeseen way is sometimes described as behaving "out of character." Such a person may even claim that he or she does not know how they came to behave in this way. "Something came over me." Everyone involved is trying to say that he or she is not really that kind of person. The point is thus missed that there is something to be understood here, and that the process of understanding is not helped by supposedly charitable euphemisms. The football manager Malky McKay was found to have sent racist, homophobic, and misogynistic text messages to a friend and colleague. When found out he said he had made a mistake for which he apologized, while insisting that he is neither a racist, a homophobe, nor a misogynist. There is no reason to doubt the sincerity of his denial. What he does not see is that, given that he wrote these messages, racist, homophobic, and misogynistic attitudes are part of him. This is what his self-image cannot allow him to recognize. Yet the behavior elicited by the stressful situation which he pleads in mitigation is part of his present identity, which he needs to understand and now has the opportunity to reflect upon.

"I am a man more sinned against than sinning": King Lear's words espouse a notion of sin that we readily understand, focusing on the harm we do to one another. But sin has been seen as primarily an offense against God: "Sin is an offence against God by any thought, word, deed or omission against the law of God" (Penny Catechism again). Of course these notions of sin are not mutually exclusive, but the whole business of sin and repentance has tended to become a transaction with God in a way that takes the focus away from the human context. Another confessional memory provides an instance. "I lost my temper with my wife," said a penitent. To the priest's question, "Have you thought of putting this right with your wife?" the man reacted with bewilderment, for in his mind the priority lay with putting the matter right with God.

A more dramatic example comes from an aspect of the crisis over the sexual abuse of children by Catholic priests. The sin was seen by a significant number of abusive priests as being primarily against God. This made it too easy to imagine that the whole thing could be dealt with in the confessional, and under the protection of the seal. This tragic divorce between the divine and the human, in which the latter is subordinated to the former, has left a trail of shattered lives in its wake. Here a distorted language of sin has become part of the problem at the very point where it is assumed to be part of the solution.

It may be said that contemporary Christianity is comfortable with a more humanly focused concept of sin, and that the divorce of which I have complained, in so far as it existed, is now a thing of the past. This may be true, but what is being overlooked here is the significance of the change for our understanding of what we like to think of as "the Christian tradition." On the other hand, reductionist versions of the concept, where sin is wholly identified with harm done to another, are also to be avoided. There is much work to be done on the largely and strangely unexamined concept of sin.

15. SEE NO EVIL

LW

IN THE TOP DRAWER of the chest where he stowed cufflinks and clothes brushes, my father kept a small brass casting of the Three Wise Monkeys. The first had its hands over its ears, the second over its eyes, the third over its mouth. As a child, they fascinated me, but it never crossed my mind that they were anything other than a solemn example, something to be imitated. This moralistic interpretation must have had to do with how I was raised and schooled.

Years later, when I was a tutor at a Church of England college, one of my duties was to deliver an annual sermon to staff and students. Just before I resigned, in the early 1990s, I preached on the theme "See No Evil, Hear No Evil, Speak No Evil." By then I had grown disillusioned with the monkeys and suspicious of their message. I accused the institution that was employing me of being too eager to condemn so-called secular society and too slow to see its own flaws. Like the monkeys, it blanked out what it could not face. There was truth in what I said, but today I can see more clearly how I was mixed up in what I was criticizing.

Although we did not use the word *abuse* back then, with the benefit of the cultural illumination that has since taken place (no thanks to the churches), I see that my target was an ecclesiastical culture that was ill-equipped to deal with the whole issue. I had stumbled across an incident that would now be classified as clerical sexual abuse. My disclosure to the bishop who should have been the responsible adult left me feeling humiliated and confused, like a naughty schoolgirl caught telling tales. He made phone calls to my superiors questioning my motives. "Leave it with me," was all that he said, and nothing was done.

The college where I taught was at the time a forcing house for the next generation of senior Anglican clergy. The regime was semi-monastic. It was a mild version of what Erving Goffman calls a "total institution." Under the cover of pastoral care and spiritual guidance, the staff had a license to look into ordinands' souls and make judgments that often cut to the quick. Some of the students could do no wrong and others could do no right. There was no effective standard or body to which anyone could appeal, and the whole setup seemed slippery and frightening. Occasionally it was downright cruel. The more mature, confident, and well-connected of the students negotiated it all with relative ease; others were harmed.

All this took place within a church in which bishops and other senior clergy could do as they pleased in the knowledge that their fellows would close ranks to protect them. Though their status was falling in wider society, they were still very much part of the English establishment. They had the right connections and a sense of entitlement to be heard, believed, and protected. Reputations would be guarded. By contrast, those who were lower in the hierarchy, both clergy and laity, could be accused of moral failings in a way that seemed arbitrary and almost impossible to counter without proving the point—that one was troublesome, disobedient, and unchristian.

It would be almost two decades after my sermon on the three wise monkeys that the extent of abuse and coverup in the Church of England started to be revealed by survivors, journalists, legal cases, and public enquiries—a nasty story that is still unfolding. As I read the official reports, I am struck by how little has changed at the top levels of church culture since I was there, despite growing awareness of the problem. The same themes are repeated over and over: abuse, disclosure by a few victims and supporters, brushoff, cover-up, silence. Today, a sticking-plaster of safeguarding procedures has become the focus, but there is still no serious attempt to look at the underlying issues.

One example will give the flavor. The Ball brothers were celebrities in the Church of England at the time I was employed there. These identical twins, both bishops clad in the cowled habits of monks, made a memorable TV spectacle. They were celebrated for their holiness and work with young people. Though it was concealed at the time, we know now that by the early 1990s those at the top of the church hierarchy knew that Peter Ball had been abusing young men in his care since the 1970s. The Archbishop of Canterbury, George Carey, was engaged in helping Ball avoid prosecution.[1] He and the Bishop of Chichester, Eric Kemp, worked hard to keep Ball out of the cells and the papers but ignored his victims' increasingly anguished

1. Gibb, *An Abuse of Faith.*

calls for help. When Ball's crimes could no longer be concealed, figures as senior as Prince Charles and a top judge interceded on his behalf. Peter Ball was let off with a police caution, asked to step down as bishop of Gloucester, given a generous disability pension and—presumably—told to keep his nose clean. He was quickly rehabilitated as an acting bishop with permission to officiate. Not surprisingly, some of his victims—who had received no apology or compensation—felt outrage and despair. Only much later did police reopen the case and bring Ball to justice, no thanks to the bishops. One victim, Neil Todd, took his own life. Ball served a short prison sentence before being released. We know now that over a dozen bishops and two archbishops—George Carey and Rowan Williams—had been made aware of Ball's crimes over the years, and that not one of them pursued the case or contacted the police.[2]

Over and over the pattern repeats itself: victims and survivors eventually tell a bishop what has happened to them, they are not listened to, and nothing is done. The institutional betrayal is a re-abuse, compounding the first. To muster the energy and confidence to complain only to be dismissed is to have one's dignity undermined again: injury upon injury. It renders the one who discloses a nonperson at exactly the point of renewed vulnerability.

The silence, the blindness, the refusal to talk—the wise monkeys are a lesson in denial and dissociation. The psychologist Carol Gilligan makes a distinction between those two: denial, she says, involves not admitting things that are plain to see—like an alcoholic denying a drink problem—whereas in dissociation we do not even know exactly what it is we have buried.[3] That may be helpful, but it is often hard to know where to draw the line. Bishops who have heard disclosures of abuse say they have no recollection—is that denial or dissociation? A survivor who disclosed his abuse to four separate bishops, each of whom denies it, tells me that "nobody can make them remember. But I will always find it difficult to believe they have no hint of memory of a significant story." Perhaps they have cut off the experience from memory and awareness, burying it alongside other unwanted and inadmissible items.

An explanation that is often given by outsiders for the churches' coverup is their concern to avoid reputational damage. That is no doubt true, but it is true of all institutions in which such things have happened. It does not go deep enough into the distinctiveness of institutional cultures. A

2. Gibb, *An Abuse of Faith*.

3. Gilligan, *Birth of Pleasure*, 169.

commercial organization covers up abuses and guards its image because it does not want to lose business and income. But for churches and their members, image can be everything. This is particularly true if they understand themselves as especially good and holy, for to lose this self-image is to lose their very identity.

George Carey and other bishops trusted the Ball brothers because they believed that bishops and monks are holy people. They represented the best and most spiritual. That meant their accusers must be the lowest. But to believe that a church and its clergy are constitutionally approved by God is a dangerous thing. Every time a church tells "secular" society how deficient it is, it reinforces the illusion. Every time it says that it is here you will find real loving community, its sets itself apart. Every time its representatives talk about "Christian love," "Christian marriage," and the "Christian family," they place themselves above reproach by "outside" standards. To admit that some of the clergy have been raping children and covering up for one another over several generations becomes impossible. Idealization and grandiosity protect against shame and guilt and play into denial.

Religions are a devil for cover stories. They are endlessly tempted to prefer the ideal to the reality, the light to the darkness, the simple to the complex. Creeds and confessions paper over complexity and messiness. People use labels like "Orthodoxy," "the gospel," and "the Christian story" to make it all more tamed and purified than it really is. Those tendencies are common, but the detail is peculiar to each institutional culture. In the Church of England, an ethos of politeness and gentility has reinforced the idea that those who don't have nice things to say should keep silent. The injunction to "speak no evil" used to be widespread in society: "watch your tongue," "wash out your mouth with soap and water," "enough tittle-tattle," "don't be dirty." No wonder some still bite their tongue rather than think or say "the worst."

I realize now that I was more enmeshed in this world than I once thought, and that it gave me a cover story, too. I was the bold young female theologian hungering for justice and "speaking truth to power." The identity of a Christian theologian and ethicist had burned into my skin, covering over what lay beneath. Now I have to ask myself why I was attracted to such a grand, patriarchal institution and why I wanted to shelter in that identity, albeit as a critic. Was I in flight from childhood experiences, seeking protection, status, and goodness? Was I like an abused wife, critical and unhappy, yet endlessly hopeful that things would change and it would be different next time? Perhaps I was so desperate to believe that the church was basically good that I could cast myself in the role of reformer in order to maintain the illusion—to have my cake and eat it too. Looking back, I can see dissociation from buried memories and shameful parts of my own life at work.

There is a need for compassion for everyone caught up in this story. People who did not fully understand about sexual abuse in the first place—and until recently that included many of us, including those who had experienced it—did not have the proper tools to deal with it. Church cultures did not supply those tools, and clerical attitudes to women and children prevented them from hearing. Some still do not want to hear, do not want to believe—they would rather cover up.

My father's Three Wise Monkeys cast in bronze turned out to be cautionary not exemplary. Closed off to sensation, static, cold, and incapable of change, they are a warning. To see things as they are rather than as we would like them to be is a useful step in dealing with what we would rather look away from, in ourselves and our institutions.

16. SAFEGUARDING WHAT?
NPH

As a result of the crisis over sexual abuse of children by priests, the episcopal leadership of the Roman Catholic Church in Britain and Ireland is now fully committed to a new system of control. There is an army of what are called safeguarding officers—parochial, diocesan, and national—whose role and work, it is claimed, will ensure maximum protection of children. The creation of this system was not preceded by any serious attention to the nature of priesthood, or to questions about sexuality and the exercise of power in the church. All that has happened is a surrender of power by bishops and religious superiors to safeguarding officers in this one particular.

In theory the role of these officials is advisory; in practice their judgment seems decisive. There is a clear logic in play. Given that bishops in general have been shown to be incompetent and sometimes worse in their dealings with abusive priests, what could be more sensible than to hand over judgment to independent experts? Furthermore, given that the earlier priority was on playing down the seriousness of the offense and its consequences, priority must now be given to the interests of those abused. This is known as the paramountcy principle, which has come to hold sway in wider society.

This latter fact has come to be adduced in defense of our new policy: at the very least we must show that we match society's rigor, if not exceed it. Yet on the issue of adoption by a gay couple the bulk of our leadership is aggressively countercultural, to such an extent that Catholic adoption agencies have either had to cease to operate or to distance themselves from the Church. For all the outstanding work these bodies have done over the years they have now been sacrificed to a high-toned stance against the societal trend. The paramountcy principle in child protection has not been subjected to any comparable critical scrutiny before becoming the cornerstone of church policy.

The Roman Catholic bishops have been panicked into a dramatic change of direction over sexual abuse alone, otherwise leaving the existing power structure and its accompanying habits of mind in place. This shift has brought to an end our former preference for dealing with sexual behavior in house. Nowadays allegations with even the slightest degree of credibility must at once be reported to the police, while the accused priest immediately departs on what is euphemistically described as "administrative leave." This entails considerable restrictions on his freedom. When the police have completed their dealings with him the safeguarding procedure comes into play, seeking to decide in view of what has come to light whether or on what terms this person should be allowed to resume ministry. Public perception is important here. The official line is that administrative leave occurs without prejudice to guilt or innocence, but it does not look so. It appears that in this one sphere the church is inclined to believe that any accused individual is guilty until proved innocent.

Of course one abused child is one too many. But injustices to abused children and vulnerable adults have been compounded by injustices to accused priests. The most remarkable feature of this story is the readiness of our leadership to sacrifice priests to the paramountcy principle, in the name of which the most elementary considerations of justice are being denied to the accused. There is a parallel injustice to those dependent on the ministry of these priests, who depart suddenly and without adequate explanation as investigations proceed. What are parishioners and friends supposed to make of this? While the sufferings of accused priests and their parishioners, relatives, and friends are not commensurate with the pain of the abused, they are not insignificant.

Along with the folly of those who refuse to believe any ill of their priest, we now have the matching and opposite unwisdom of seeing any hint of abusive behavior through the lens of a one-size-fits-all reductionism. The tendency is to regard anyone who has ever done anything that comes into this category as thereafter, and forever, a danger to children. In the present climate any hint of abusive behavior, of whatever kind and however long ago, induces a readiness to believe that the suspect is a serial predator on the watch for further opportunities. Allegations against priests, not surprisingly, cover a wide spectrum of sexual behaviors, many from a long time ago. Yet the ill-informed mantra persists that any such behavior indicates an addictive pattern which, if not incurable, is at best extremely intractable. It is hard to ensure a hearing for those experienced observers who know this is far from true.

It might well have aroused suspicion, but does not seem to have done so, that an authority that for so long has practiced concealment and denial in a form that often precipitated further abuse should have been so suddenly converted to aggressive safeguarding. What has happened is that our leadership has opted for the easy course of procedural rather than fundamental reform. Furthermore, the safeguarding process is extra-canonical, so that it lacks the checks and balances of a well-established legal system. Much in canon law is designed to protect the interests of the individual, but there appears to be no appeal to those provisions from the findings of the safeguarding officers.

This observable readiness to allow canonical provisions to be set aside suggests what is really happening. The previous policy of sacrificing children's well-being to the maintenance of the Church's good name has been replaced by the sacrifice of accused priests to the attempted restoration of that name. A dominant factor has been a concern with image rather than substance. The crisis is seen as something to be managed rather than as an opportunity for creative learning. In theological terms the chance of further conversion of the Church is being missed. When news of priests and religious abusing children first became a headline, bishops began to say that we must make the Catholic Church an example of best practice in this matter. These remarks demonstrate the same overriding concern for the image of the Church that drove the earlier and now discredited policy. The preoccupation seems to be with how, having failed so abysmally, we can now show ourselves in the best possible light. This is not to say that there is no concern for children, but that such concern is clearly not the driving force.

Sexual abuse by priests is approached as if it is a thing on its own, which can be stopped by an exemplary procedural rigor. Our Church is now committed to treating the most horrifying symptom of what is wrong as if it is itself the disease. But a cautionary note is in order here. Unhelpful as the Church's current attitude to accused priests may be, it is also unhelpful to demonize seemingly negligent or unfeeling bishops and religious superiors. These men should rather be seen as largely having conscientiously followed the norms of the organizational culture of the Church. That they have done so is precisely the trouble. (On this point, as for much else in this chapter, I am indebted to Marie Keenan's book, *Child Sexual Abuse and the Catholic Church: Gender, Power and Organisational Culture*.)

What we have in the Church is an abusive power structure, not just particular acts of abuse and cover-up. This is what is so intractable. What else can explain the blindness of a pastorally-minded person like Cardinal Sean Brady of Armagh in saying, "I did what I was supposed to do," when he failed to take responsibility for his knowledge as a young priest of Brendan Smyth's behavior? Brady's response in interviews precisely exemplifies Marie Keenan's observation that the organizational culture of the Church undermines moral responsibility. At the time he even assured the abused children that the matter would be dealt with and swore them to secrecy, while doing nothing beyond reporting his findings to the bishop.

In the Catholic system an ordained priest has no real accountability to those he serves. A power trip is always on the cards, facilitated in this regard by the inadequacy of canon law, and still more by the infantilization of the laity that characterizes our Church. Given that sexual abuse is commonly in part an abuse of power, it has found a relatively favorable ethos in our priesthood. Still on the theme of power, the crisis is much more about inadequate and misguided oversight than it is about abuse as such. It is fatally easy to lose sight of this in the midst of understandable, justified revulsion at particular abuses. It gives the worst possible signal that bishops such as Cardinals Bernard Law and Cormac Murphy-O'Connor, whose earlier attitudes led to horrifying abuse, continued to be honored by the Vatican and in the Church at large. The former presided, until his retirement, over a Roman basilica, and remained a member of several Roman dicasteries. The latter was appointed by the pope to head up the apostolic visitation of the archdiocese of Armagh following revelations of clerical sexual abuse in that region. You couldn't make it up!

I spoke to someone who was brought up in the parish of the Norbertine priest Brendan Smyth, who became the most notorious of the serial abusers of children among the Irish clergy, ending his days in prison. "All the children knew what he was up to," said my informant. "Well armed with sweets, he tried it with everybody. We did not tell anyone. We were afraid of the priest, and afraid to tell our parents because in their eyes the priest could do no wrong." In the comparable case of Sean Fortune in Wexford it seems that grownups did know something, for there were jokes about the priest's proclivity, but nobody was prepared to take responsibility by taking the matter further. Passivity and deference remain factors in the continuance of clericalist domination of the Church.

It is beginning to be recognized that research into the childhood experiences of perpetrators and a recognition of the importance of treating the victim in the perpetrator are key to understanding child abuse. This is an invitation to think beyond the Manichean categories of abuser and abused, as if individuals can only be one or the other. As long as the Catholic authorities continue to give absolute priority to the paramountcy principle this humane perspective can find no place. This principle militates against justice by absolutizing one element in the situation, namely the supposed welfare of children, as if this can be adequately considered apart from everything else. This insight in no way lessens the seriousness of sexually abusive behavior, but suggests a context in which it can be understood and guarded against with the cooperation of the offender. While it may be true from a social work perspective that there are situations in which appeal to the paramountcy principle can be defended, it should not have become a rule of thumb for the Church in its quest for renewed respectability. Meanwhile there is no alternative to the present ruthless scapegoating of abusers as long as fundamental questions about priesthood, about sexuality, and about power are not revisited.

17. THE NEW EVANGELIZATION
NPH

THE "NEW EVANGELIZATION" BEGAN in the time of Pope John Paul II and was vigorously promoted by his successors. It is an ongoing project in the Catholic Church enjoying considerable support. The assumption behind the movement is that, because of its history, Europe is still the heartland of Catholicism. It is powered by a second supposition, that there is a serious crisis of belief and practice that, if not soon reversed, can end only in a catastrophic collapse of faith and therefore of the Church. All hands to the pumps, therefore, to avert such an outcome. The project is the attempted re-conversion of those we used to call lapsed Catholics. The adjective "new" is emphasized to distinguish this form of evangelization from the more traditional attempt to draw unbelievers into the Church. The term is sometimes given a much looser meaning which is not, directly at least, the concern of this chapter.

There is an element of cultural imperialism in the suggestion that Europe is still the decisive factor. No serious attempt is made to justify this view. Something similar can be said about the alleged nature of the crisis. Is it really a crisis of faith? It could rather be an observable waning of allegiance to particular forms of belief and practice that no longer hold people or that they have outgrown. This alternative analysis recalls Teilhard de Chardin's disagreement with Pope Pius XII's claim that the world is divided into those who believe in God and those who do not so believe. Teilhard's idea was that the divide was rather between those with a sense of becoming and those without such a thing. This sounds better in French, but the distinction is between those who see the whole thing as in process and those who think in more idealized terms.

There is no rigorous scrutiny in this project of what it is to be lapsed. The old Catholic habit of mind continues to prevail that mass attendance is the decisive indicator of faith. A connected point is that the New Evangelization takes it for granted that we know what is in the best interests of the lapsed. This is dramatically demonstrated in the prayer prescribed by the Catholic bishops of England and Wales to be recited at mass each Sunday, under the revealing heading "Coming Home": "We pray for everyone in our parish community, that they may find the right words and means to invite our absent brothers and sisters to return to the practice of their faith." All that is desired here is a return to a pre-existing state of affairs, without any sense of growth or development. It is hard to avoid the conclusion that at least unconsciously we want the lapsed to be no more than copies of ourselves, confirming by their return the wisdom of our allegiance. Another way of putting this is to say that the church has difficulty in accepting the human environment of the convert. It is worth noting in passing that St. Paul spots the same tendency in himself—"I wish that all of you were as I am" (1 Corinthians 7:7). For him, this consideration is inconclusive, but the New Evangelization seems not to share this restraint.

The approach is oddly un-relational: for any creative human interaction each participant needs to be open to the possibility of receiving something from the other and being thus changed. A one-way transaction such as that envisaged by the bishops' prayer is necessarily sterile. What the lapsed have learned beyond the confines of the Church cannot be ignored without mutual loss.

The New Evangelization assumes that those who give up regular Catholic practice go to something of less worth. This is an arbitrary assumption. Gavin D'Costa, a theologian from a strongly Catholic background, told a conference on the New Evangelization that his sister had recently become a Buddhist, thereby becoming an even better person. He was by no means suggesting that it is absolutely or inevitably better to be a Buddhist than to be a Catholic, for he himself remains the latter. His point was a more subtle one, and it is significant that those commending the New Evangelization had nothing to say in response.

The Second Vatican Council represented a revolution in Catholic attitudes to other churches, other faiths, and those belonging to no faith. But it is seldom realized how much this plays back into what it means to be church. Once the boundaries are less tightly drawn and those we used to generically call non-Catholics are seen in a more positive light all notions of evangelization must be called in question. Receptive ecumenism implicitly recognizes this in the interchurch context, but the insight needs to be broadened out into the wider world to have its full impact.

The problem is the imperialistic tendency of Catholicism to hold that our revelation is definitive and complete. In this way we disable ourselves from appreciating and responding positively to the much larger, messier, more many-splendored world that lies about us. Islam, too, claims an absolute and universal truth; and it should be noted that these two faith traditions also share a long association with forms of empire.

My parish priest in Handsworth, the most multiracial district of Britain, reminded us in a Christmas sermon that "the whole world has come to Handsworth." That is the big picture. The sting in the tail was his next observation that out of all the immigrant groups we had only got as far as relating to the most recent, the Vietnamese, and that because they were Catholics. At present this pattern can be seen repeating itself in the suggestion that in the face of the present refugee crisis we should give preferential treatment to those who are Christians. Some Catholic bishops in Eastern Europe are even saying that they are the only refugees we should admit. It has been suggested that it is against the interests of our faith to facilitate the entry of Muslims and unbelievers to Europe because to do so threatens to undermine the work that has been done in building a Christian civilization. The Polish bishops headed up a crusade of praying the rosary around the entire borders of their country for the protection of the nation. In view of the ongoing furor against Muslim immigrants in particular, and the event being arranged on the anniversary of the Battle of Lepanto, there can be no doubt against whom this crusade was directed. Such attitudes are part of the context, more sociological than theological, within which the New Evangelization must be seen.

The overarching impression is of a project uncomfortable with the labor of ongoing interpretation of creed and tradition, particularly in the light of historical criticism and contemporary experience. A parallel and connected point is that those who think like this are less than honest about the scale and depth of intra-Catholic disagreement. In relation to the visit to Britain in 2010 of Pope Benedict XVI, then the leading advocate of the New Evangelization, a movement called Catholic Voices was founded to train young people to give a certain kind of answer to difficult questions about the Catholic Church. It was reported in the press that when Martin Pendergast, a Catholic who publicly takes a positive approach to homosexuality, wanted to attend a meeting of this group for the sake of balance he was prevented by the organizers from doing so.[1] This demonstrates that

1. Butt, "Catholic Church caught in new row."

movements of this kind are sectarian rather than Catholic in that they proceed in defiance of the wide range of opinion within the church.

True evangelism entails further conversion of the Church, and perhaps the most serious charge against the New Evangelization is its tendency to minimize if not to ignore features of the Church that drive people away. Each of us might have our own checklist here, and emphases will of course differ in accordance with personal circumstances and history. The nearest the New Evangelization gets to recognizing this is in cosmetic notions of making our parishes more welcoming, without any serious thought as to why they are not so, still less any real reflection on the substance of belief. It is presumed we have the package the lapsed need. It can be readily acknowledged that evangelizers are driven by a sense that they are obligated to seek out those who are seen as "distanced" from the Church. This conviction follows from a particular understanding of the Church, and in that sense has a moral underpinning. But questions of security and identity should not be ignored. Religion is far from exempt from what the *Observer's* Andrew Rawnsley once called, in the context of the meteoric rise of the Scottish Nationalists, "the magnetic power of the politics of identity."[2]

2. Rawnsley, "Scottish Nationalists."

18. IN DEFENSE OF
THE INDIVIDUAL

LW

WALK INTO ANY CHURCH on a Sunday morning and you may well hear a sermon about the dangers of modern individualism. Society, it will be said, has become atomized and fragmented, community and cohesion are vanishing, loneliness is the modern disease. Modern men and women have become too autonomous, too selfish and, well, too individual. The solution is church—a loving community that stands against the tide of individualism.

Intellectually this approach gets encouragement from the communitarian strand of modern philosophy and theology. John MacMurray popularized communitarian thought in Christian circles in the midtwentieth century and was cited by Tony Blair as his favorite philosopher.[1] Alasdair MacIntyre's *After Virtue* (1981) excited theologians with the suggestion that modern societies had been rendered morally incompetent by their atomized individualism and that the cloistered communities of Benedictine monasticism were the best hope for the cultivation of virtue. Charles Taylor's *A Secular Age* (2007) contrasted the "buffered" modern secular self unfavorably with the more open and "porous" self of traditionally religious societies.

Inspired by such thinking, the liberation movements in Christianity that flourished in the 1960s and 1970s fell out of fashion as theology took a more conservative turn after the 1980s. Labels like "black theology," "womanist theology," and "liberation theology" were used to marginalize and set them apart from "orthodox," "radically orthodox," and "postliberal" forms of theology. One of the doyens of postliberalism, Stanley Hauerwas, sums up his program in the course of attacking the liberation theologian Gustavo

---

1. Baggini, "Blair's Philosophy."

Gutiérrez: "As Christians we do not seek to be free, but rather to be of use, for it is only by serving that we discover the freedom offered by God."[2]

The more we learn about abuse and its effects, the more flawed these postliberal and communitarian approaches appear. For what makes abuse possible, and its effects so damaging, is the fact that its victims are so *unbuffered*, so permeable, so trusting of religious communities and their leaders. Stephen Bernard, an Oxford academic who as a young man was repeatedly raped by his Catholic priest Canon Thomas Fogarty, observes in his memoir: "Fogarty was 'in' me in a physical sense, but he was also 'in' me in a psychological sense. There was something full and all-invasive to his violation of me which it is almost impossible not to admire."[3]

It is because we are social beings, shaped and made by others, that we can be unmade and undone as well. By the same token, those who perpetrate abuse often seem to be "made up" by their exercise of dominating power—they steal something fundamental from their victims. Every night, Bernard reports, he has to write himself notes so that on waking he can read them and remind himself who he is.

Postliberalism makes a useful point when it criticizes inflated ideals of selfhood and independence. But it is not helpful to confuse such extravagances and distortions with a proper regard for individual freedom. As the struggles of abuse victims and others show, winning a good-enough degree of confidence and self-acceptance is for many of us a precious, fragile, and hard-won achievement, not a dangerous temptation. It involves traveling through layers of shame and facing up to dissociation from painful memories. "There are mothers," reflects Deborah Orr in her autobiography *Motherwell*, "who will never cease to refuse their daughters their own identity, in whatever way they can."[4] The least the liberal project aims for is a defensible sense of self that grounds the right to stand up to a difficult parent, or to tell a tormentor to piss off.

What postliberals dismiss as selfish individualism is sometimes what psychotherapists celebrate as "individuation," the easily disrupted process in which we grow, through dependence, towards creating a uniquely personal way of being. We only become less porous because we began by being very porous indeed. Relationship is important, but so is what Virginia Woolf calls "a room of one's own." "At the centre of each person," said the

---

2. Hauerwas, *After Christendom*, 53.

3. Bernard, *Paper Cuts*, 31–32.

4. Orr, *Motherwell*, 103–4.

psychologist Donald Winnicott, "is an incommunicado element, and this is sacred and most worthy of preservation."[5] Too much community and conformity can result in the creation of what Winnicott called a "false self" that is pleasing to dominant others but fatal to spontaneity, honesty, and a sense of being truly alive.

We are simultaneously fascinated by free spirits and troubled by them. Postliberal ambivalence about freedom is understandable, but why baptize this fear? Why the preference for "servitude" and "being of use," as Hauerwas puts it? Of use to whom? Hauerwas would say: of use within the body of Christ, the church—but we know now how horribly that message can be abused. Feminist, black, and postcolonial theologians who have been pointing out the unequal and unfair treatment of women and black people for many decades sound an important warning. The lessons have still not been learned. The ready scapegoating of allegedly evil individuals is no substitute for rigorous scrutiny of harm done in the name of institutions and communities.

The irony is that Christianity played an important role in the historic development of liberalism over many centuries.[6] The liberals and liberationists that postliberals attack have as great a connection to tradition as they do. It is no more "orthodox" to dismiss liberal strands of Christian thought than to celebrate freedom as a Christian value.

Church leaders only approve of freedom selectively. It is hedged around with qualifications like "his service is perfect freedom"—as if it were a dangerous thing that needs fencing in. Pope John Paul deplored calls for women's liberation while energetically campaigning for freedom of religion. This ambivalence extends to interpretations of Jesus. Sometimes he is presented as a unique individual who defies the authorities to forge his lonely path, at others as a model of obedience.

From the insight that we are social creatures, it has been too easily concluded that we should belong to tight-knit religious communities. That message is catnip to churches anxious to boost their numbers. Even evangelical Protestants are busy creating new kinds of "cell" community, while Catholic bishops look to tight-knit lay movements (under episcopal oversight) as the best hope for revitalization, and Anglican bishops give up on parishes in favor of "worshipping communities." Whether they are speaking of the Focolare movement, Verbum Dei, "Bash Camps," Opus Dei, the Jesus

---

5. Winnicott, "Communicating," 187. Cited in Phillips, *Winnicott*, 3.

6. Siedentop, *Inventing the Individual*.

Army, Holy Trinity Brompton, or house churches, there is a naïve assumption at work that just because they are pious they can be innocent of abuses and power plays. Those who lauded an idealized version of monasticism have now to face the findings of public inquiries that reveal shockingly high levels of abuse and cover-up in many such communities across the world. The strategy of idealizing Christian communities and then defending them to the point of cover-up cannot be justified by elegant theology.

Instead of glorifying certain sorts of Christian community as unique enclaves of loving community, it is more realistic to think of churches as junction points where traditions and practices, the living and the dead, the human and the divine, the earthly and the heavenly come together in a myriad different ways, both good and bad.

It may rightly be said that "liberalism" can be turned into an ideology just as "communitarianism" can. When this happens they become artificial opposites, tokens in a pointless war. The concept of liberalism is more helpful where it is less ideological and invokes pragmatic institutionalized protections that protect individuals and individual freedom from forces that can easily overpower them. Child protection ("safeguarding") is one example, democratic arrangements and human rights are another. Overarching such protections is the liberal preference for the kind of pluralism that allows individuals to belong to many different communities simultaneously, enslaved by none.

It is thoughtless to assume that we have all achieved the state of being confident, free individuals. Freedom is a process that has to be worked through again and again, generation after generation, life by life. The supports it requires are unequally distributed, and those who access them most freely have no business denying them to others. It is often said that liberal Christianity has failed—but it is not clear that it was ever really tried at the highest levels of church leadership. It remains an aspiration.

19. PRAYING FOR THE DEAD
NPH

"It is a holy and wholesome thought to pray for the dead, that they may be released from their sins." My Catholic upbringing in the 1940s emphasized this, and recommended a range of religious practices to this end. Any sense of grieving for a lost loved one was complicated by anxiety about that person's fate in the next world. My purpose here is to examine subsequent changes in the approach to death.

The form of Catholic belief and practice that characterized my childhood was not unusual among British and Irish Catholics at that time. The basic picture was of a struggle to avoid sin, and to pursue appropriate remedies as and when sin was committed. The deathbed practice of the last rites (confession, extreme unction, and communion) was intended to maximize the person's hope of a not-too-unfavorable outcome of the judgment that was thought immediately to follow death. The likelihood, it was supposed, was a period in purgatory, which could be shortened by the prayers of repentant sinners for the one who had died. The souls in purgatory were destined for heaven. That was why they were designated as holy or faithful, as in the prayer commonly said for the recently dead and on anniversaries: "May their souls, and the souls of all the faithful departed, through the mercy of God rest in peace." For the unfaithful departed there was no hope, this tradition being explicit about the ineluctable fate of those who died in mortal sin. More of that anon, but what was not emphasized was the difficulty of committing mortal sin, given the rigorous terms in which it was defined. Our teachers seemed most concerned that we should never at any moment take it for granted that all was well with us, or with the deceased.

Commended above all other good works was an act of perfect contrition, which would bring about the cancellation of the entire burden of the punishment an individual had incurred. Nevertheless such perfection was deemed to be unlikely in the contrition of most of us most of the time, and in any case only God could judge whether the required standard had been attained. So a host of other practices were recommended with a view to more modest outcomes. The task of doing what we could for the purgatorial state of those who had died remained incumbent on all. Except in the case of those beatified or canonized by the Church it was recommended that all should be prayed for, since any deceased person could be in purgatory and therefore in need of our prayers. Particular prayers and pious practices, known as indulgences, were judged to be especially efficacious in reducing someone's time in purgatory. A tortuous explanation was offered as to how the phrase "temporal punishment" could apply in an extraterrestrial setting.

It is curious that the doctrine and practice of indulgences survived so strongly into the Catholic world of my childhood. When Luther raised his battle cry the Vatican was well aware that the doctrine of indulgences did not rest on the firmest foundations, and so moved the debate on to the question of papal teaching authority. When these disagreements hardened into institutionalized ecclesiastical division indulgences survived, and were even perhaps given a new lease of life, by becoming part of a package of things considered intrinsic to Catholic orthodoxy. New thinking in this area, initially not at all confined to Luther and his disciples, was in this sense a casualty within Catholicism of Reformation conflict and the resultant aggressive/defensive stance taken by the Roman Catholic Church.

There is an amusing sequel to this part of the story. When the Anglican-Roman Catholic International Commission agreed statement on justification by faith first appeared some Anglican evangelicals smelt a rat, reasonably enough, because it did not address the question of indulgences. I was present at an official ecumenical gathering at which several Roman Catholics were uncomfortable that this criticism was made. The reason for their discomfort was that they knew the doctrine and practice of indulgences had not gone away, but they did not regard the matter as of crucial importance, and certainly did not relish engaging in the defense. This kind of embarrassment was already a far cry from my childhood world, to which incidentally a somewhat coy throwback was provided by diocesan bishops' letters, written presumably under orders, designating certain local churches for obtaining the Jubilee indulgence promulgated by the pope in 2000. I wonder how many English Catholics took up the offer. How many would have noticed if it had not been made?

What change in the attitude to the dead is indicated by the waning of concern for the obtaining of indulgences? The obvious thing to say is that the change in question is part of the purported distancing of death in Western culture: religious thought and observance are not immune to major cultural trends. As far as it goes this is a neat explanation, and probably not without some truth. But it begs the prior question as to whether the theory of indulgences still widely practiced in the Roman Catholic Church earlier in the twentieth century was an appropriate theological response to the phenomenon of death. Regardless of what has happened since, it is hard to regret the passing of a sin-centered and punishment-fearing theology of death. Those black-bordered cards giving notice of someone's death, and including an indulgence prayer and the number of days obtainable by reciting it, projected an image of God that now looks distinctly quaint if not sinister. It needs of course to be remembered that indulgences were not about forgiveness: they offered "remission of the temporal punishment due to sin after its guilt has been forgiven." Nevertheless the focus was on sin, and on a God who seemed extraordinarily preoccupied with our misdeeds and those of the deceased.

It is worth noting that the idea that everything would be put right elsewhere, when it was most strongly held, was accompanied by a highly colored picture of an eternal hell that did not lack inhabitants. The satisfaction that even the most sophisticated medieval minds appear to have taken in contemplation of this, as a vindication of divine justice, is not something we readily share. It may be that our age, with good reason, is newly aware of the abiding ambiguities of all our lives. Within the kind of innocence that stops short of this awareness, hell may have served as somewhere to put those people, or even those aspects of ourselves, with which we could not cope. As such it does not work, for they do not cease to be part of us. Belief in an eternal hell, however passionately held, resolves nothing in our relations with the dead. To see hell as the ultimate destiny of wicked dictators—or, as Dante did, of bad popes—is an attempt to vindicate a sense of justice, but on our terms. It is in one sense a relief, though an illusory one, not to have to think about such people, still less to pray for them.

If the practices resulting from the doctrine of indulgences now seem a radically inadequate way of commemorating the dead, it would be lamentable if their disappearance were to be succeeded by nothing. But this seems improbable, given the depth of our involvement with those who have died. There is no reason to suppose that we lack the resource to find new ways, just as those who still prefer the old ways sustain them regardless of what liturgical purists say. Candles are still lit at side altars during the celebration of mass. It is doctrinaire, especially in things that touch us so intimately, to insist that there is only one right way of communicating with the dead. Cultural developments do not happen tidily, in immediate or obvious sequence with what went before. We have to live with a certain insecurity in this as in other matters.

The present marginalizing among Catholics of an indulgence-based approach to praying for the dead makes room for a quite different sense of our continuing involvement with them, one which keeps the best but avoids the worst of the earlier approach. People commonly think about the dead, so that it would in any case be rash to suppose that ceasing to pray for them means that we do not take them seriously. The issue is often confused by uneasiness about the predominant tendency at funerals to "accentuate the positive," to eulogize the deceased if at all possible, giving uncritical thanks and praise for this person's life. This trend risks leaving no place for the often profoundly conflicting memories and feelings that commonly characterize bereavement.

Contemporary funeral practice too often assumes that the departed one is already with the Lord in a way that places him or her above or beyond the ongoing struggle in which we are all involved. A funeral liturgy that invokes resurrection in a ritualistic way can only offer a bland image in face of the complex spectrum of emotions and reflections undergone by bereaved people. Appeal to resurrection faith in an attempt to transcend the ongoing negotiation of our relationships with those closest to us among the dead begs all the questions. Some people imagine that with the death of a difficult parent or an estranged spouse they will be free. The subsequent realization that this is not so can be chastening, but is a step out of unreality. From this point of view the notion of purgatory as purification might still find a place, no longer in penal terms but as an attempt to recognize unfinished business between the living and the dead. Was this perhaps the kind of thing our forebears in faith were trying to say?

Since the context of a significant death is always one of relationship, it is nonsense to suppose that anything in need of resolution between two people can be fully dealt with in one while remaining unresolved for the other. To think thus is to reduce the whole transaction to a kind of atomized individualism. A healthy corrective is provided by a prayer in the Greek Orthodox liturgy for the Virgin Mary that is doubly remarkable since it comes from a tradition that exalts her as the Mother of God. The underlying sense is that no individual, not even the Mother of God, is completely fulfilled until all are fulfilled: all are in need of prayer until the consummation. Discomfited by the prayer, some scholars have argued that this version is a mistranslation, but that view has not prevailed. Western devotion to Mary has idealized her, giving her so privileged an intercessory role on our behalf that her solidarity with us in unfinished business is not usually considered. Such an exalted intercessor, it is supposed, cannot herself be in need of prayer. This misses the crucial point that no individual can so utterly transcend his or her community. An acute christological question immediately arises, for if this is true of Mary what must be said of Jesus?

The form of exaltation of Mary exemplifies a wider point about attitudes to the dead. We tend either to idealize (as with Mary) or to demonize (as with Judas Iscariot) those who have died. It is convenient to do one or other of these, with a view to covering up complexities and ambiguities. Such a cover-up is not necessarily conscious, but there is a price to be paid. There is always a danger that by way of idealization, demonization, or oblivion the relationship becomes fixed at the time of the person's death. Insistently reverential attitudes and practices in connection with our dead may themselves be no more than forms of avoidance or denial.

Another way of looking at this theme is to note the contrast between the language of praying for the dead and the language of praying to the saints. In our old religion the dead were thus neatly divided into those who needed our prayers and those whose prayers we needed. There were those dead who were in effect dependent on us, and those on whose patronage we were dependent. This categorization now seems at odds with that sense of mutual dependence in relationship which characterizes the modern Western outlook. It would be easy to mistake this move away from a hierarchical way of seeing the matter for lack of interest in or concern about those who have died.

Could it be that the language of praying for or to the dead has proved too constricting? The waning of these practices may indicate a creative dissatisfaction with the forms of relationship implied by them. Our involvement with the dead is not primarily about needs, whether theirs or ours. It is about an ongoing communion which looks to the consummation of all things. Intense concentration on what is proceeding in this world does not distract from or compete with attention to those who have died once it is realized that these relationships continue in the form of remembering.

To avoid any suspicion of a one-way process here it is worth reflecting on the arresting statement of some postmodernists that "the past remembers us." This hint of a disturbingly unfamiliar perspective may help to break down a narrowly linear view of time that otherwise may dominate and impoverish our awareness of connections with the dead. Be that as it may, the processes of this remembering, which change the relationships involved, do not require the positing of some other world in which the departed may or may not be flourishing. There is quite enough going on here, where awareness of the dead can change dramatically as our own lives proceed. By contrast, the preoccupation with the states of life of individuals in some other world which they are supposed to have entered by death is hardly life-enhancing.

There are forms of remembering that are prior to and more foundational than any petitionary activity. The suggestion that the key notion in relation to the dead is remembering rather than praying might be taken to imply the end of theology. Instead it is worth reflecting for a moment on the eucharistic prayer, in principle the supreme act of remembering. Anti-Protestant polemic has so insisted that it is not merely a memorial that this characteristic is easily underplayed in Catholic contexts.

In this connection, we can ask what devotional forms might help to interiorize our sense of our communion with the dead. For example, what kind of prayer best fits the dynamic of remembrance that constitutes our continuing engagement with the dead? If it is true that we shall be saved together or not at all, then the prayer must be for and with everybody, for no individual's flourishing is separable from that of the others. Looked at like this a prayer for another or others is indivisibly a prayer for myself. It is a prayer of and for the communion which is in the making. (This is a comment on what is happening when people pray for the dead rather than an argument against the practice.)

Remembering, then, is central. There are, however, pitfalls here, for our culture tends to think of memory as providing a less reliable equivalent to a video or tape recorder. On this view the machine tells what really happened. But neither memory nor machine works like that. Appeal to either necessarily entails selection, interpretation, reinterpretation according to what is of present significance. Frank McCourt has been accused, no doubt in some sense justifiably, of making up the conversations in his memoir of childhood, *Angela's Ashes*. Yet the writing is so vivid and immediate that someone was led to comment that you can almost smell the particulars of the tale. The narrative historian C. V. Wedgwood has pointed out that there is no such thing as the bare facts. We need to be aware of this when proposing memory as the central category for our present connection with those who have died.

Does serious remembering of the dead depend on belief in some sort of life after death, and in a world other than this one? Some Christians would answer yes, and go on to insist that only some such belief can give point and purpose to our life now, and in particular to our hope for one another. But as Karl Marx among others saw so clearly, such convictions can easily be escapist, and pious hope of a world other than this may serve as a device to avoid taking responsibility in the world as it is. Meanwhile Freud said that the human unconscious lives as if it is immortal, a statement which leaves open the possibility that the notion of another world that we enter on death is a fantasy. Instead of rushing to the defense of traditional formulations against these so-called masters of suspicion, we need to ask what place the idea of life in another world after death really has in our lives, what urgent claim if any it makes on us, and how it plays out in our relations with the dead.

I can only say that a brush with a potentially terminal illness and the major surgery that followed gave me a much heightened consciousness of the preciousness of the present, while leaving me agnostic about any sort of afterlife. It was not that I came to disbelieve in it. I discovered that it had no purchase on me. Against all my religious upbringing, in particular its sacramental aspect, and to my own quiet surprise, I felt no need to prepare except in a practical sense. A friend has pointed out that as it was the pressing thought of imminent judgment that had ruled my tradition, the key thing was the lifting of that anxiety. Yet my conviction about our involvement with the dead is unchanged. I am in no doubt that we are all, living and dead, bound up together in a communion that is in process of formation and transformation.

Yet none of this need point in the direction of a world other than this one. When I was taught, as mentioned above, that heaven is not a place but a state, it was still strongly implied that heaven is not here. But why not? Whether the ecstasies that have come your way are mystical, aesthetic, sexual, political, or whatever, they qualify for the language of heaven much more vibrantly than artistic and literary efforts to offer images of heaven in another world. Aquinas's high talk of the beatific vision that awaits us does not make it inviting. And if you find no ecstatic experience here, why should you suppose that it will be available to you elsewhere? This world, I should prefer to say, is heaven in the making. If the language of process is taken seriously there is no need to posit two worlds, but to those who think only in terms of states this assertion will be meaningless or unbelieving.

Strong interest in life after death is not a notable feature of contemporary Christianity. The considerations just advanced militate against the notion that this has to do with avoiding the thought of death. In face of a newly sharp and immediate sense of my own mortality I found myself with a more vivid and uncluttered grasp of the present as sheer gift than I had ever had. A diminished concern about the afterlife may well be the accompaniment of a much richer awareness of the wonder of this universe and its possibilities. The dead are not distanced or forgotten when anxiety about their fate has no place. They have their part in the emerging communion, and there is of course communication with them, unless we have become amnesiac.

There is much to be said for the view that only in coming to terms with one's own mortality is it possible to be fully alive in the present. The mistake is to suppose that such coming to terms equates with belief in an afterlife. Clearly some form of self-transcendence is desirable, and such experiences seem not uncommon. But it may well be alienating rather than life-enhancing to tie this aspiration too tightly to the notion of some other world that we enter by way of death, and to locate the consummation there. How many of us can say, hand on heart, that we are stirred or inspired by such a belief? The answer we give to this question has important consequences for how we think about and pray for, or to, or communicate with, the dead. Any view of death that takes the edge off life in the present is to be resisted as a flight from reality. Christians are ready enough to criticize reincarnation as an escapist idea, but are often reluctant to apply comparable critical rigor to their own convictions.

Taken-for-granted ideas about afterlife in another world are just as likely to be a denial of the reality of death as is a refusal to think about death at all. If there is unreality here so will there be in every aspect of our involvement with the dead, however much we conscientiously call them to mind, praying for some and to others according to longstanding Catholic custom. Equally unreal is an insistence that this world is all there is, when by that is meant a world in which possibilities of transformation are not taken seriously.

Mention needs to be made of the fact that traditional Christian prayers for the dead are made in the name of the risen Jesus, on whose behalf the claim is made that he did not remain "among the dead." To labor a point that is less obvious than it might first seem, that is very different from any suggestion that he did not die. It is also very different from the suggestion that at some point after death he resumed the previous form of his companionship with his own, for that would mean that he had not really died. His death meant that that chapter in their relationship with him was over, and forever. There is no going back, as is made clear by the wonderful story of the angel with a flaming sword guarding the gate of Eden against the possibility of re-entry. That prohibition of regression, painful at times though it is, is in our best interests. This point was missed by a parish priest who rebuked a widow for having her husband cremated. His grounds were that she had thus prevented her husband's resurrection. On the other hand, there is no reason to suppose that the resurrection is a statement about an afterlife in another world. The image of bodily resurrection, it seems to me, has to do with a rearrangement of the furniture of this world. As such it is a sign of hope indivisibly for the living and the dead, not a glib or shadowy assurance that everything that is out of order here will be put right elsewhere.

In many traditional religions there is a strong sense of the presence and power of the ancestors. To try to imitate this in any direct or immediate way would be to decontextualize these religions and thus to romanticize them. But the analogies between some of the ways Christians think about Jesus and so-called ancestor worship deserve further exploration. Our childhood catechism asked the question, "Where is Jesus Christ?" and gave the answer that as God he is everywhere, but as man he is in heaven and in the Blessed Sacrament of the Altar. We were not told where heaven was, although the implication was that it was a very long way from where we were, or from anything within our experience. Elsewhere it was said that heaven is not a place but a state, an observation that seems to come from a different universe of discourse. The point for our present purposes is that the catechism was extremely cagey about the presence of Jesus amongst us. This nervous insistence that Jesus was only to be found in one hallowed and rigorously controlled sacramental practice suggests an underlying uneasiness about our communication with the dead, which is not allowed to provide a natural and even obvious context for his presence with us.

I shall be told that modern theology and catechesis have moved on, and that in any case the resurrection of Jesus makes him available to us in a way quite different from and superior to that of other ancestors. This claim to superiority, commonly advanced by Christian theologians by way of the coded phrase "the uniqueness of Jesus," is in reality a power claim and needs to be recognized as such. Perhaps it is enough to point out here that the fashionable kenotic christology that stresses the self-emptying character of Jesus' story does no more than what preceded it to promote a lively awareness of our involvement with the dead. It makes of Jesus such an omnicompetent co-sufferer as to dehumanize him, demonstrating that the attempt to make him everything succeeds in making him nothing very much. It may be that the resistance to allowing Jesus to take his place as an ancestor springs from a fear that to categorize him thus would threaten the distinctiveness of our convictions about him. Yet if he is not this, he has no human context and can play no part in our remembering those who have died.

Placatory prayer for the dead, along with its accompanying practices, is no longer apposite. It reflected a fearful, sin-centered image of God and his relations with us, including those who have died. It imagined two worlds, rather than one world in process of transformation, thus promoting a dualistic understanding of what it is to be human and therefore of the state of the dead. It was individualistic, focusing on each in an unrelated way, as if the well-being of our dead could be secured in an atomized, piecemeal manner and regardless of what was happening to us. Finally, placatory prayer does not reflect a proper sense of our involvement with the dead in a developing communion, fostered by creative remembering and looking to an unimaginable consummation. This is what now seeks devotional expression, and it remains to be seen what will emerge. It is no use waiting for the Vatican—but devotional life has never found obstructive officialdom an insuperable obstacle.

20. RESURRECTING RESURRECTION

LW

As THE CONFIDENT SECULARISM of the twentieth century recedes, the dead are coming back to life. Secular scientific approaches segregated the dead from the living; bodies were removed from homes, periods of mourning shortened, continuing bonds with the dead pathologized, and grief allocated set stages aimed at "closure."

In the new millennium much of this has gone into reverse. Surveys show that beliefs in both an afterlife and a soul have been growing steadily in Britain since the 1950s, while a study in the USA finds that the largest increases in belief in life after death "are among the least religious Americans and among subgroups that have not traditionally emphasized an afterlife."[1] Funerals are being reinvented and dead bodies are being handled in new ways. At a recent annual funeral exhibition I noticed that the most popular stand was one selling shrouds—rough canvas bags designed to replace traditional coffins or caskets. What appealed was not just the low cost but the fact that you could make out the shape of the dead body under the shroud: "It seems more real," several people told me.

At the same time, traditional Christian belief in resurrection has been falling steadily. Since it cannot be blamed on declining interest in the afterlife, it is to how resurrection has been presented that we must look to explain its eclipse.

The so-called "doctrine" of resurrection has never been as clear, uncontested, or unchanging as that way of presenting it implies. Lack of agreement is already evident in the New Testament. The Gospel of Mark in its earliest known versions has no resurrection appearances at all, only an angel and a promise to three women that he is not here in the ground,

---

1. Voas and Chaves, "United States a Counterexample," 1524.

but you will find him where you live your lives, in Galilee (16:1–8). It would no doubt have suited some early Christian interests to have had an instantly recognizable and unambiguous Christ rise from the grave, proclaim his divine credentials to large numbers of people, confer authority upon a select group of representatives, and ascend to the Father. That is indeed the picture that churches in subsequent centuries often tried to paint, and it is echoed in New Testament scholarship that pays more attention to Jesus' resurrection appearances to men than the finding of the empty tomb by women.[2] But the Bible preserves a more interesting variety of memories and perceptions that convey a sense of the strangeness of a "risen" Christ who defies expectations and transgresses neat divisions between the living and the dead, the human and the divine, the this-worldly and the other-worldly, the spectral and the real.

In the New Testament stories, Jesus, after his death, appears only a few times to only a few people. At first they do not recognize him. This ghostly figure can do strange things like pass through walls, appear and vanish—but also cook fish and invite Thomas to feel his wounds (John 21:9 and 20:27). Paul falls from his horse, hears a voice, and is blinded (Acts 9.1–9). This risen Jesus is not a man brought back to life like Lazarus, for if that were so there would be no difficulty recognizing him. As it is, Mary mistakes him for the gardener and the disciples on the road to Emmaus walk and talk with him for miles without suspecting who he is. There is continuity with the man from Nazareth crucified on a cross, but strangeness and discontinuity too.

Resurrection hardly appears in the Hebrew Bible, and it was still controversial in Jesus' time. The New Testament reminds us that the Pharisees accepted it but the Sadducees did not. Where it is found it is often tied up with a wider millennial or apocalyptic expectation that we find in many religious traditions. In Jesus' day this was often part of a hope that the God of Israel would intervene in history to vindicate the chosen people who were suffering under Roman rule; so when the idea of resurrection was applied to Jesus, these associations came with it. This is why Paul speaks of Jesus as the first-fruits of a general resurrection that God will bring about at the end of time. This catapults Jesus to the heart of millennial expectation, for if raised, he must be central to God's plan to redeem the world. This is an important step in the creation of what would come to be called "Christianity"—an imperial religion with an enormous sense of purpose

2. Schüssler Fiorenza, *Jesus*.

and an urgent message for the world, sometimes backed by violence. In an emerging orthodoxy, the future of the world would come to hinge on this God-man and "his" church.

We have already come a long way from the empty tomb tradition. But even in the context of ecclesiastical consolidation, the meaning of resurrection was never fully settled. Questions remain. What happens to those who die before the Day of Judgment? Will there be one resurrection or two? How does belief in resurrection relate to belief that the dead go immediately to heaven (or hell)? What sort of a thing is the resurrected body?

There is a long and unresolved debate in Christian history about whether resurrection is bodily or spiritual. In Stanley Spencer's paintings the dead clamber heavily from their graves dressed in their Sunday best; in other depictions they are angelic beings floating around in a heavenly realm. Augustine insisted that resurrection involves the reconstitution of flesh and bones. In *The City of God*, he tries to answer some of the questions this raises: how old will our resurrection bodies be? (his answer: thirty-three years old) and what if I am missing an eye or a limb (his answer: bodily perfection will be restored).[3] Today the tendency is for the guardians of orthodoxy to insist on a "literal" bodily resurrection, but no one refers to Augustine's struggles to spell out exactly what this means. "Don't ask too many questions" seems to be the prevailing attitude. Perhaps it is part of what made the doctrine of resurrection seem so unhelpful to many modern people dealing with bereavement.

It is impossible to have an open and imaginative discussion about resurrection when it is treated as a doctrinal shibboleth. I have heard many sermons in which the preacher declares complete assurance about "the" resurrection—left unexplored and unexplained—and insists that it must be the heart of our faith, too. The preachers are using resurrection as a battering ram to prove Christian supremacy and draw a line between faithful and unfaithful. Paul is cited in support: "if Christ has not been raised, then our preaching is in vain and your faith is in vain" (1 Corinthians 15:14). But the letter to the Corinthians in which this verse appears shows that there were alternative views: "How can some of you say that there is no resurrection of the dead?" (1 Corinthians 15:12) asks Paul, coming down hard against the skeptics and ending with fearsome eschatological warnings about the subjection of all things to God and the destruction of all enemies, including death.

---

3. Augustine, *City of God* (XXII, 15, 19) 1055-56, 1060-62.

It is not only Christians who can be dogmatic about death and what happens after. The novelist Susan Hill recalls that her two most staunchly atheist acquaintances, Susan Sontag and Christopher Hitchens, had the greatest difficulty in dealing with their own deaths. This she ascribes to an "intellectual arrogance" that prevented them from even contemplating the idea that there might be a spiritual dimension to life, death, and after-death. "An open mind," says Hill, "is surely best in the face of death, because intellectual pride and arrogance, and how your fellows, who hold the same position, think of you, gets you nowhere. Belief, admitting the possibility of another dimension, of a spiritual side to humanity, is no more of a sure thing than negativity, but at the very least it is a comfort—and what is wrong with that?"[4]

As belief in resurrection has faded, we find ourselves floating in a rich soup of ideas, including reincarnation, heavenly reunion, and eternal souls. This is the context in which the dead are coming back to life. The anthropologist Martin Stringer finds that many people entertain a raft of these apparently incompatible beliefs, because after all "we don't know for sure." But his gentle probing discovers coherence beneath the surface, for individual accounts make sense of different facets of a person's engagement with death: reincarnation for self, heaven for reunion with loved ones, angelic existence for those who feel like guardian spirits.[5]

The Harry Potter novels offer a vivid exploration of relations between the living and the dead and reject resurrection on moral grounds. Individual bodily resurrection is depicted not as hope but as temptation. When Harry throws away the resurrection stone at the end of the *Deathly Hallows* he rejects what it offers in order to be truly human. For the generations raised with these books, these stories can be as vivid and meaningful as the book of Revelation for some of their forebears—and what is wrong with that?

Decline in resurrection belief may also be due to a sense that it is undermined by discoveries about cosmology and evolution. If we no longer believe that the world and human beings were created fully-formed by God at the start, it is less plausible to think that there will be an ending and a re-creation at the end—a general resurrection. Finger-snapping events of instantaneous creation have given way to ideas of process and evolution. The more we understand ourselves as evolved, social, and encultured "creatures

---

4. Hill, *Jacob's Room*, 109.

5. Stringer, *Contemporary Western Ethnography*.

of our time," the less easy to believe in re-creation at a future point: in such a different context would we not be different people?

There are more immediate existential problems, too. What do you say to a bereaved child who asks, "Where is Mummy or Daddy, or Ruby the hamster?" or to a parent who asks the same about their child. The churches have always struggled to answer. Hope of resurrection at some unspecified future date does not help when the question is "where is my darling now?" or when someone feels the presence of the dead or sees a ghost.

Tony Walter, a sociologist who studies changing attitudes to death, thinks these failures of theology help to explain the recent growth of alternative popular "theologies" in Britain. He traces how belief that the dead become angels has grown in popularity in recent times.[6] I see the evidence around me. In my local cemetery and public country park there are benches engraved with the names of the dead where you can sit to be close to them; little windmills to catch their presence; angel images and poems to memorialize them. Walter suggests that these are tentative and pragmatic post-Christian ways of articulating ongoing relationships with those who have died, and coping with loss and change. Perhaps similar beliefs have always been around, but the rolling back of Christian as well as secular-materialist ideas has allowed them to come into the open and develop.

By presenting the resurrection of Jesus as an event of unique importance, different from all else, Christianity may have made it seem irrelevant to "ordinary" experiences and concerns. The ban on praying for the dead, the denial that the risen Jesus is anything like a ghost, the ridicule of spiritualism and mediums, and the hiatus between death and judgment, led to disconnection. What got left out was a way to connect the original experiences of Jesus' resurrection with ours. Although resurrection belief may reassure some believers that they are on the right side of history, it drains the stories of their power to connect the living with the dead here and now. How ironic that Jesus' resurrection, so transgressive of the boundary between the living and the dead, became a barrier that kept them apart.

Reading the New Testament accounts again, I see something different. I approach the texts through my experiences and stories, personal and collective, because that is our only way in. What strikes me now is that without the women and men to whom Jesus appeared we would have no resurrection at all. This does not imply that they made it up. They were human beings who had experienced a traumatic death in which their hopes had been

6. Walter, "Angels not Souls," 31.

shattered. The work they had to do to turn that experience into something lifegiving cannot have been wholly unlike what we all do in the face of a searing bereavement. And if that is so, those stories are still engaging as we live in the presence of the dead. There is no "closure" in the apostles' bereavement experience, so why should there be in ours?

The nineteenth-century spiritualist William Denton invited readers to imagine two "worms" or caterpillars, folded in their cocoons, wondering whether there is to be any future life for them. "I have an idea," says one, "that I shall fly when I have eaten my way out of this case in which I am enclosed." That is all nonsense, says the other: "Worms we are, and worms we must ever be, and now are shut up in what must, in the nature of things, be our grave."[7] The kind of resurrection belief I was taught supports the second worm but adds: "But at the end of time Christ will return to raise you from the grave, a resurrected worm." This is significantly different from the picture that another Christian, William Blake, engraved of a caterpillar and chrysalis with a human face, signifying the transformation of the human soul at death.

It is through my immersion in the cultural soup of today with its mixture of beliefs in angels, butterflies, spirits, and ghosts that I reconnect with the variety in the Bible and other Christian writings. It opens up the meaning of resurrection and gives me a sense of the profound transformation involved in all dying and "rising," and of how ongoing relationships with those who have "passed over" transform the living, too.

---

7. Denton, *Is Spiritualism True?*, 22. Cited in Schlieter, *What Is It Like to Be Dead?*, x–xi.

21. THE LURE AND CURSE OF ORTHODOXY

NPH

> We would rather be ruined than changed
> We would rather die in our dread
> Than climb the cross of the moment
> And let our illusions die.[1]

THE OPPORTUNE DISCOVERY OF Linda Colley's book *Captives* provides a leitmotif.[2] Colley offers an account of Britain's pursuit of empire and how its soldiers and civilians "were held captive by the dream of global supremacy." The fashionable critique of empire builders has to do with the harmful effects of their policy on those they colonized. Without denying those effects Colley's theme is the quite different, though related, one of how the colonizers were themselves held captive by their dream.

So it is, I suggest, with the notion of orthodoxy. The claim to a divinely validated, trans-historical, and universally applicable truth appears to offer security and empowerment. The thought is captivating in both senses of the word. There is a heavy price to pay in terms of repression, exclusion, and denial of personal responsibility if this dream is to be sustained. As with the empire, the gap between the dream and the resources available to sustain it becomes imprisoning. In his 1993 encyclical *Veritatis Splendor*, Pope John Paul II sought to establish the concept of exceptionless moral norms but ended in the fallback position of an appeal to the charism of truth residing in his office. In his Regensburg address of 2006 his successor, Pope Benedict XVI, told us that the only happy marriage between faith and reason is to be found in his version of Catholicism. All else, within and outside the Church,

---

1. Auden, *The Age of Anxiety*, "Epilogue."
2. Colley, *Captives*, 76.

is unreason, with the potential for violence. Theologians and philosophers such as Étienne Gilson, Alasdair MacIntyre, John Milbank, and Catherine Pickstock have all pursued sophisticated versions of the Regensburg line. Each in their own way was attempting to keep the dream of orthodoxy in business. The empire builders' dream of global supremacy foundered on the hard fact of a small island's limited resources. Here it is a matter of a necessary impoverishing of the available intellectual and spiritual resources in order to sustain the theological dream.

A priest friend of mine said recently that people have a right to know what the authentic teaching of the Church is, as if such a thing were readily and unambiguously available. A document from the Catholic Bishops' Conference of England and Wales in 2004, *Cherishing Life*, sought to provide a summary of such teaching in the field of sexual and medical ethics. Acknowledging disagreements, they argue that as successors of the apostles they nevertheless have a duty to tell us what the teaching of the Church is. This seems to me one of many instances in the life of our church where allegiance to orthodoxy leads to irresponsible behavior in the form of disengagement from living questions. The document treats the teaching of the Church as something out there, a kind of take-it-or-leave-it entity that admits of no serious discussion and is quite unrelated to any notion of learning. A long and varied tradition of ethical enquiry is reduced to a ready reckoner set of truths to which decisive appeal can be made.

The Catholic Church's International Theological Commission told us in 2013 that heresy has been present from the beginning. What this means is that we have never been as certain as we would like to think, but have always struggled to acknowledge this. Pope John Paul II's long list of heroic apologies for wrongdoing by our Christian forebears stopped sadly short of saying that we as a Church got it wrong. For instance, despite the evidence, he could not or would not say that we were a Crusading Church. It was only individuals who erred. Yet a striking feature of the Crusading movement, as of Catholic antisemitism, was the way in which it ran through the Church from top to bottom. It was a pervasive spirit in our religious culture, which went far beyond mere individual fault. Failure to recognize this is a dramatic instance of orthodoxy's power to imprison: it cannot have been the case that we were a Crusading Church, or indeed an antisemitic Church, because neither is what the church is.

The Catholic Church, like other churches, it seems to me, is constantly changing, while never admitting it is doing so. So the claim persists that we are doing no more than presenting the same old doctrines in new ways. It is not uncommon to find tortuous euphemisms used in these debates, not least by those who as orthodoxy's victims judge that the price of forthrightness is too high. They may themselves also still be captives of orthodoxy in the other sense. An example is the Church's teaching on religious liberty. We were against it until Vatican II, but have been in favor of it since. Joseph Fuchs remarked in *Christian Morality: The Word Becomes Flesh* that the tortuousness of the document of the Second Vatican Council that declared the change results from the conciliar fathers' reluctance or inability to admit that a change of mind had occurred. Thus obfuscation results from a compulsion to preserve at all costs the assumption of an underlying, unchanging orthodoxy. A historical perspective would have suggested that while the Church was in a position to influence or control by political means what was to be believed it saw (or at least took for granted) an advantage in not yielding anything to the cry for religious liberty.

Aquinas defended the burning of heretics for the common good! Now that Christians in some parts of the world are under threat from other dominant groups, the Church changes its tune. There is also the example of North America, where a form of Catholic belief and practice can be seen to have prospered without any special backing from the state, and comes to support such "religious freedom." In terms of how human groups tend to behave this change is perfectly natural, though perhaps long overdue: but what it puts under extreme strain is the idea of a reliable authenticity of teaching.

Two kinds of question are involved in this discussion. One is about identity. The human craving to be somebody, or at least something, commonly finds a religious focus. The concern for consistency and continuity in Christian belief and practice can often be understood as rooted in this craving. A particular and strongly held religious allegiance can provide a seemingly firm sense of belonging to a cohesive group. The other area of questioning here is epistemological, concerned with what kind of certainty, if any, we can have. A preliminary point to note is that the "revealed truth" to which religious people tend to appeal is a kind of shimmering orb that lacks definition.

Various strategies are in common use to sustain the notion of orthodoxy. First comes the appeal to the Bible, considered as the inspired word of God that provides the basis of the church's teaching on both faith and morals. The eclectic nature of the books of the Bible does not deter adherents of this approach from treating it as in principle a seamless garment. Even the most distinguished theologians are not above using dubious rhetoric to distance themselves from the consequences of studying these texts as the product of other times. Karl Barth, who recognized the problem, argued that "if we have a particular interest in antiquities, we read (the Bible) . . . at the risk of failing to serve even our own interest and missing the real nature and character of the writings." There is, he insisted, "a Word within the words," thus in effect evading responsibility for his own interpretations.[3]

Recent advances in textual criticism have also brought more clearly into view the extent to which we mislead ourselves by thinking of a text (in this case the text of the Christian Bible) as an object rather than a process. "The beguiling format of the book, so evidently a thing that we can see, touch, caress . . . or burn out of hatred . . . leads to the text and the work it represents becoming an object. But the object, the copy, is only a tiny part of the process which is the work."[4] Textual critics have repeatedly been accused of providing stumbling blocks for the faithful and ammunition for the impious. As late as 1881 Westcott and Hort, themselves very distinguished critics, felt constrained to say that there was "not a single theologically motivated variant reading in the New Testament."[5] On the contrary, textual variations attest to a continuing interest in adapting the text to make it better serve current theological concerns. In this respect, allegiance to orthodoxy clearly imprisoned these great minds. My suggestion is that once we take textual criticism fully seriously the Bible as foundation stone of orthodoxy disappears.

It may be said in response that it is not so much the teachings of the Bible as the mind of Christ, made available to us through the Bible, that provides the touchstone of orthodoxy. In biblical interpretation before the modern era the hermeneutic key to unlock the meaning of both Old and New Testaments was the assumption that every biblical text expressed in some way the mind of Christ, pointing us towards that understanding of himself that Jesus intended we should have.[6]

Versions of this approach persist in both widespread popular and more scholarly forms. A speaker at a theological conference said that unless there is substantial and identifiable continuity between the self-consciousness of

3. Cited in Jungel, *Barth*, 76.

4. Parker, *Textual Scholarship*, 21.

5. Cited in Parker, "Textual Criticism and Theology," 325.

6. See O'Loughlin, "Christ and the Scriptures."

Jesus (meaning who he supposed himself to be) and orthodox christology the game is up. The statement was rhetorical, as the speaker seemed to be in no doubt that such continuity could be easily shown to have existed. In that sense the game *is* up, for we cannot be certain what Jesus' mind *was* about himself. All available evidence suggests that each culture and age constructs versions of Jesus in the light of its own intellectual and moral concerns and esthetic preferences. Groups quarrel over the validity of particular constructions, each thinking theirs is the right one.

Then there is the appeal to tradition. P. J. Fitzpatrick in his book *In Breaking of Bread* makes the point that whereas Catholic Church leaders have at last begun to take serious cognizance of biblical criticism, they are far from applying such methods to other major documents of church history. This move would be far more threatening to certain forms of Catholic identity than would any amount of biblical criticism. Fitzpatrick writes of a past that is "revered but unsatisfactory" and draws attention to the technique of "'supervenient isolation," used as an attempt to circumvent the difficulty. A particular statement is plucked from a document to validate a modern claim; but insistence on proper contextualization soon exposes strains and even contradictions between what was being said then and what we might want to say now.[7]

It is sometimes said that the Catholic Church has a duty as well as a legitimate concern to define its boundaries as an intellectual community. Why? How much of our past would we have to exclude to make this task of boundary definition manageable? How could we complete the job without the arbitrary exclusion of much that in its own day passed for orthodoxy? Tradition is a living conversation. Much is filtered out, sidelined, or ignored as the conversation proceeds. But that process is quite different from the attempt to exclude on some a priori intellectual ground anything that might be thought. The insistence on boundaries springs from a concern with identity and power, not theology.

History is full of the stories of those who have proclaimed their way as the only way, to the exclusion of all others. None have prevailed enough to make their claim convincing. Heretics and their descendants have not been sufficiently cowed or persuaded, even by force majeure, to abandon their convictions. Nor have they in their turn been tolerant of diversity. In seeming contrast an ecumenical age may look to what different Christian groupings have in common rather than to what may divide them. But today's

7. Fitzpatrick, *In Breaking of Bread*, 228.

professional ecumenists, like their intolerant forebears, take for granted a core of belief and practice, though they cannot agree on its constituents. Their hope is that all interested parties will come to acknowledge and give their allegiance to the supposed core.

Newman, who knew enough history to recognize that the teachings of the church have changed, appealed to the notion of development. However, difficulties arise with the attempt to say what constitutes a development rather than a deviation. Where would we find a frame of reference which would make such judgments possible and reliable? Appeal is commonly made to scriptural, credal, and other traditional documents. But once it is understood that these sources are themselves manifestations of Christianity's process of continuous revision the task of distinguishing true from false versions becomes intractable. If on the other hand we employ criteria of judgment independent of these sources, which in practice is what largely happens, we are allowing ourselves to be guided by an authority outside the tradition in reaching conclusions as to what to take seriously. Thus the appeal to development does not avoid the danger of equating orthodoxy with the old Soviet line: orthodoxy is what we, the leaders, say it is today. All concepts of development are coercive. The truth shall set you free. Not documents, not formularies, but the truth.

When I first proposed these ideas in public someone pointed out that tradition means, or at least entails, the handing on of something. Indeed. But in what form, and with what consequences, does this handing on proceed? If tradition is a living, continuous conversation we are inescapably and helpfully in touch with our own past. But the illusion that we are or could be bound by it is the dream of a total, monolithic truth already established and divinely guaranteed. The consequences are dire.

An example from history may serve as a warning: Cardinal Reginald Pole, Mary Tudor's Archbishop of Canterbury and right-hand man in her attempted restoration of Catholicism. Between the trial and execution of convicted heretics Pole insisted that they were to be exposed to sermons exhorting them to forswear their errors. To us this might look like a form of psychological torture, but Eamonn Duffy insists that Pole's motive was benevolent: he wanted to give these wretched, misguided people a last chance to avoid eternal damnation, a fate which would surely follow if they were to die unrepentant.[8] But Pole was a man of high culture, deeply imbued with the humanism of the day, and he was one of a significant number

---

8. Duffy, *Fires of Faith*, 150.

of leading ecclesiastics who had come to see that Luther was more right than wrong about justification by faith. This conviction became harder to sustain as the Church became more polarized against the Lutherans, and Pole in consequence came close to a breakdown. Having been summoned from exile to Mary's side, he felt compelled to see the Catholic version of absolute truth through right to the end. In denying his own unresolved inner conflict Pole became a persecutor, but one who offered his victims one more chance of salvation. How had he negotiated this conflict within himself? History does not answer this question.[9]

In contrast to attitudes shared by all sides at the time of the Reformation, modern Christianity acknowledges a need to engage seriously not only with variant forms of the tradition but also with other faiths. Multifaith dialogue is, in theory at least, the order of the day. But the consequences of this are not yet being faced, especially the fact that such an engagement cannot be fully serious unless the Christian's conviction is allowed to be questioned by the other person's belief. The claims made by another tradition cannot be properly attended to unless the possibility is granted that this meeting will change, perhaps radically, the form of my appropriation of the Christian tradition. Some Christians claim that such encounters confirm them in their own belief. This suggests a certain complacency, equivalent to saying that I am untouched by the mysterious reality of the other person.

In *When I Was a Child I Read Books*, the American novelist and essayist Marilynne Robinson tells us that over the years of teaching and writing she has tried to free herself of "constraints I felt, limits to the range of exploration I could make, to the kind of intuition I could credit."[10] She came to see that religion "could and should disrupt these constraints, which amount to a small and narrow definition of what human beings are and how human life is to be understood." Robinson admits that religion often fails to aspire to this aim and task, and is even hostile to it. To my mind this links with the fact that some of the most searing rhetoric in the New Testament is directed against those addressed as "blind guides": "You traverse sea and land to make a single proselyte, and when he becomes a proselyte, you make him twice as much a child of hell as yourselves" (Matthew 23:15).

An underlying preoccupation of this chapter is with the question: "What drives the state of mind of those who resist all change in matters of religious belief and practice?" In pursuit of this and kindred questions I

9. This reflection owes much to the historical expertise of my sister, Dr. Margaret M. Harvey.

10. Robinson, *When I Was a Child*, 3.

have found the following oddments illuminating. They are offered here in no particular order and with some glossing from me.

Sebastian Moore suggested a dramatic answer: fear of the void.

Anthony Kenny, once a Catholic priest, is quoted in Magdalen Goffin's biography of E. I. Watkin, as saying that had the papacy changed its mind on contraception Catholic belief would have lost all credibility.[11] That supposition is what seems to have swayed Pope Paul VI in his decision to maintain the prohibition. Yet a friend of mine who has since become a bishop voiced the diametrically opposed conclusion that without an early change in this teaching credibility will soon disappear. These two sharply conflicting opinions pinpoint orthodoxy's dilemma.

It has been argued that adherence to a rigid orthodoxy is a sign not of faith but of its opposite. This opens up an intriguing possibility. In the Catholic weekly *The Tablet* Clifford Longley wrote: "What modern Catholics most lack is the permission to be spontaneous and creative, to be allowed and encouraged to think outside the box (to use the modern jargon). We are too afraid we might be getting it wrong, which leads to a host of other mistakes that one might term neurotic super-orthodoxy."[12] Where neurosis prevails faith is the casualty.

Relevant here is the monk-poet Kevin Maguire's poem "Faith."

The trees move in the wind and are alive,
Though rooted in the ground they grow.
But oh the men, the faceless men
Who have built themselves a monolith,
Intricately carved and beautiful,
To possess which is all
(To doubt it is catastrophe):
Why are their faces so grey and stony,
Filled with nameless fears,
Bloodless and arid as trees seem in the winter?
But the green giants are growing,
And the sap is rising;
And even the roots of trees
Can overturn a stone.[13]

11. Goffin, *Watkin Path*, 266.
12. Longley, "Mozart," 7.
13. Maguire, "Faith," 53.

The psychotherapist-writer Adam Phillips draws attention to "the unspeakable cruelty people are capable of when they are sufficiently credulous to act on behalf of an absolute truth."[14] This capability is writ large in history, but my interest here is in what such people are doing to themselves.

Since our claim to absolute truth is in an important sense untrue the strain on those charged with sustaining it is unimaginable, and does not dispose them for rational and proportionate responses to current crises. Instead of blaming them for the patent inadequacy of their responses, we should be doing all we can to relieve them of such an intolerable burden. But if any such thing is to happen we must first do what we can to rid ourselves of the grandiose expectations that the modern Catholic Church has tended to place on the papacy. "The fault, dear Brutus, is not in our stars but in ourselves, that we are underlings."

In the end the captivity of orthodoxy is the state of mind of those who feel unable to pursue living questions wherever they lead. That state in its turn means that we cannot take responsibility for our own lives and for our world.

14. Phillips, *On Balance*, 116.

22. THE IMPLICIT GOD OF CHRISTIAN ETHICS

LW

"ALL ETHICS IS THEOLOGICAL." This refrain in contemporary Christian ethics is intended to make the point that, since such ethics flow from theological presuppositions, the task of the Christian ethicist is just as theological as that of the systematic theologian. Although this may be nothing more than a salvo in an academic struggle over status, it can also serve as a useful reminder that Christian ethics carry implicit understandings of God. Sometimes the assumed deity is at odds with the one who is consciously and explicitly invoked: a ghost at the theological banquet listening quizzically to the rhetorical constructions being made about him (or, rarely, her or them).

I have taken part in several ecclesiastical and theological consultations on "Christian anthropology." They all understood their task to be giving an account of what it is to be human from the perspective of Christian faith, with a concern to counter other understandings and reflect upon threats to human flourishing. From their own standpoint this seemed uncontentious, yet there were huge assumptions and submerged messages. The chief one was that it is possible to know what it is to be human, not just in scientific terms but in normative and metaphysical ones. One can put the skeptical emphasis at any one of four points here: that *we* can *know* what it *is* to be *human*.

Assumptions go all the way through: that there is a special knowledge possessed by the experts; that this knowledge of the human condition is extensive, reliable, and universal; that there is one way of stating truthfully who and what we are; that the human is an unproblematic category distinct from other animals and objects; that there is a singular Christian view to be found and stated afresh.

Christian ethicists might object that they are not necessarily assuming any of these things, and they willingly admit the limitations of creaturely knowledge. Some have been doing important work on animals and "post-human" themes.[1] There are also new discussions about epistemology. But when I was involved, I constantly ran up against the assumption that, whatever our human shortcomings, theologians have special access to truth by way of Scripture and incarnation. Not by reason then, but by revelation. Thus, certain presuppositions of Christian ethics and moral theology set the terms of our debate in a way that was not open for discussion. We gave fealty to a wise and benevolent Father God who always knows what is best for his children. He is the sensible, ordering, all-knowing, dependable one on whom we can always fall back. He is the reasonable guarantor of order and meaning, who reveals his intentions, through Jesus Christ and the Scriptures, to the scholarly gaze. Here is the authority figure to whom we refer back for guidance. He reveals what it is to be human.

But the more I engaged in this work, the more uncomfortable I became with the assumption that we had a special and privileged access to normative knowledge. I comforted myself by saying that it did not mean I was any better than the next person at living my life. But I could not deny the implicit claim to power, about which there seemed at that time to be little professional reflection. We might think we were striving honestly to witness to God's truth, but our "vocation" as moral theologians carried a powerful implicit message about our status and authority over others (who were assumed not to have vocations, at least not like those of clergy and theologians). Like our implicit God, we were setting ourselves up to pronounce and judge. Saying that we were ourselves sinners just made things worse, setting up a defense against looking honestly at what might be going wrong.

I was struck then as I am struck now by how an implicit God of Christian ethics emerges from the work of even the more radical exponents of theological ethics in spite of what they say explicitly. Let me illustrate the point with two celebrated theological figures a generation apart: Dietrich Bonhoeffer and Stanley Hauerwas. Each is regarded as pioneering and bold, each is aware of the sorts of issues I raise. If Christian ethics can carry other conceptions of God besides the paternal authority figure I have described, it is here we might expect to find them. In fact, we find something much more ambivalent. The medium seems often to militate against the message or, more accurately, to throw up different and contradictory messages.

1. One of my favorite examples is Wallace, *When God Was a Bird*.

At one level, Bonhoeffer is deeply aware of the sorts of implicit messages that Christian ethics can carry. In the *Ethics*, he scorns the "pharisee" who uses ethics to exercise power over fellow human beings. He takes seriously Nietzsche's insight that Christian ethics is often propelled by resentment or what we would now call passive aggression. He paints the true life of discipleship as one in which good deeds flow directly from the divine life in which the Christian participates, not one in which we use principles to judge others and ourselves. Bonhoeffer celebrates the freedom of a Christian to live not as an obedient slave but as a creative and responsible adult whose life is renewed by faith. In the *Letters and Papers from Prison*, he speaks of a new ethic for "man come of age," and in keeping with its fragmentary, occasional, and personal form, he gives the impression of speaking from his own human standpoint rather than on behalf of God, *sub specie aeternitatis*.

And yet that is not the whole story. For there are other elements of Bonhoeffer's work that convey a very different message about God as father figure and judge on high. Included in the *Letters and Papers* is a wedding sermon that begins by affirming that it is "by their own free and responsible action" that the bride and bridegroom have come to the altar and "conquered a new land to live in." Reassuringly, it says: "They have been given such immense freedom and power to take the helm in their life's journey . . . we ought not to be in too much of a hurry to speak piously of God's will and guidance." But then comes this: "to put it more exactly, you, Eberhard, have all the responsibility for the success of your venture . . . and you, Renate, will help your husband and make it easy for him to bear that responsibility, and find your happiness in that." Lest there be any doubt Bonhoeffer adds: "You may order your life as you like, except in one thing: the wife is to be subject to her husband . . . . The place where God has put the wife is the husband's home."[2]

What Bonhoeffer gives with one hand he takes away with the other: the freedom of a Christian, the dignity and responsibility of humans before God—but only for men. The message is bolstered by the medium: the theologian-preacher lays down the law from the pulpit and tells the couple and the congregation what is good for them. He speaks on behalf of a God as powerful and uncontestable as the ethicist himself, and there is no room for reply.

2. Bonhoeffer, *Letters and Papers*, 43–44.

What Bonhoeffer says in this wedding sermon does not drop out of the skies. It is part of his appropriation of a Lutheran ethic of God-given "orders" or orderly spheres of human living. For Luther, marriage is one of the spheres God has ordained for the living out of a properly human life. So it is for Bonhoeffer, and so it is for his God. It is not to be questioned any more than the preacher is to be questioned, for to do so would be the very kind of disruption the orders are set up to guard against. The preacher's authority to speak, to name, and to command is a prerogative deriving from creation, in imitation of the creator himself.

There is a similar tension in the virtue-based communitarian ethics of Stanley Hauerwas. One of its most attractive features is its unsystematic, discursive, and occasionally autobiographical style. It eschews the moral high ground and engages with novels, sermons, congregations, and everyday life. Yet, as with Bonhoeffer, there is a discordant message. Hauerwas also draws back from the full implications of what he is suggesting. Some voices feature much more prominently than others and white, male, heterosexual authority is enforced through references, bibliography, quotation, imagery, tone, and example. This tension characterizes virtue ethics more generally: on the one hand rejecting deontological command ethics and the dictator God they imply; on the other striving anxiously to name and contain what counts as virtue and vice in ways that privilege those who name and exemplify these things over others. Below the surface variety in Christian ethics, it is disappointingly common to find an implicit understanding of a commanding omni-God that is widely shared, rarely acknowledged, and highly contentious.

It is noteworthy in this context that the "content" of modern Christian ethics and preaching has thinned out in modern times. Concrete moral guidance and condemnations feature less prominently than abstractions about love, community, covenant, peaceableness, and so on. This leaves Christian ethics in a dangerous state: with a condescending and dogmatic approach but little to offer by way of concrete guidance. It raises it to a level of incontrovertible abstraction. What is missing is detailed attentiveness to the particularities of our situations. Perhaps that would require much greater engagement with ordinary life and a renunciation of the illusion that the preacher or academic has some special moral insight about it.

Thankfully, there are some hopeful examples of approaches that are more willing to engage with real life, less closed to non-Christian sources, more self-critical about Christian forms of authoritarianism and mind control. Some kinds of practical and pastoral theology have moved in this direction. And there are Christian ethicists who sit on expert bodies making moral discernments about concrete issues in open conversation with people of other kinds of religious and non-religious conviction. Here ethicists take responsibility rather than hiding behind higher authority.

The challenge is for theology to think of God other than as a superhuman authority at the top of a pyramid of moral authority in which women are above children, men above women, clergy above laity, church above other faiths (and none), and Him above all.

23. PRINCIPLES—THE ENEMY
OF MORALITY

NPH

THE APPEAL TO UNIVERSAL principles in moral matters is pervasive, not least in a Christian context. In his push for moral renewal a previous Archbishop of Canterbury appealed to the ten commandments and the teaching of Jesus, while the then Cardinal Archbishop of Westminster awaited an authoritative ruling from Rome. The underlying state of mind is the same in each case: an insistence that there is available a comprehensive set of principles which will give us, always and everywhere, reliable guidance as to how we should conduct our lives. Both leaders looked to something oracular to remind us of these principles—in the one case the Bible and in the other the Vatican—and to guide us in their application. Each takes for granted some underlying principles as the foundation of moral living.

Two questions arise: where do such principles come from, and do they significantly help our moral decision-making? As for the second question, such principles were clearly no help to Adam and Eve as they began to explore the possibility of a more differentiated and responsible identity than they had known in their infantile life in the garden. What use were principles to Abraham, faced with the Lord's command to kill his son Isaac, the child of promise? How was Moses helped by principles when invited at the burning bush to turn his life upside down in the interests of a project so unbelievably at odds with his present responsibilities? What principle drove Jesus to reject out of hand the anxious concern of his mother and other family members and friends, who sought to save him from himself? What principle brought him to the cross, which Hebrews tells us he endured "for the joy that was set before him"? We are told that "greater love has no man than this, that a man lay down his life for his friends" (John 15:13). How does such a principle find application in the actual death of Jesus? There is no evidence that the situation suggested to anyone involved at the time that it was a loving act to put himself in danger as he did.

Again and again in the Jewish and Christian traditions choices are made that have nothing to do with moral principles. What is at issue is the possibility of conversion into a more many-splendored and ambiguous reality than the seemingly tidy and secure world of principles. This conversion response is not so much against principles as aside from them. Yet to continue to cling to principles when we are invited to take a step beyond them is to refuse the adventure of faith. It is in this spirit that Kierkegaard insists in *Fear and Trembling* on the necessity of the suspension of an ethics of principles in the interest of faith in the living God, universal principles being an alternative to such faith. Bonhoeffer found himself surrounded by pious, principled people who colluded with Nazi rule in Germany. In deciding to engage in the plot against Hitler's life he did not claim that this involvement, including of course a whole web of deceit, was an example of good or right action. That would have been to concede too much to the mental world of principles that he had come to see as unregenerate.

Long ago I told a fellow monk that I had decided to leave the monastery. "I could never go back on my vows," he said. Implicit in this was a clear statement of principle, that vows are to be kept. His words showed me that it was not like that for me, although I had taken final vows without any mental reservation. At this later moment the vows had gone; imperceptibly they had ceased to have any purchase. I saw that vows do not have a timeless and universal objectivity. They have meaning only in a context, which in my case had ceased to exist, although the externals remained the same. There is a moment in Evelyn Waugh's *Brideshead Revisited* when the narrator, a committed soldier, recalls the time when "love died between me and the army."[1] That is it exactly, and when that happens it is time to go, lest corruptions befall. My colleague was interposing the vows as a static and unchangeable entity between himself and the Spirit, as do proponents of the indissolubility of marriage. How seriously I had previously taken the vows is shown by the following epitome of my state of mind early in the novitiate: "I don't know what this thing called monastic life really is. Please tell me and I will do it." That is a state of mind in which principles are everything, a condition already morally desensitized to the human particulars, terrifying in its avoidance of reality. It is reminiscent

---

1. Waugh, *Brideshead Revisited*, 3.

of Strelnikov's approving remark in the film of Pasternak's *Doctor Zhivago*: "The Revolution has destroyed the personal life."[2]

As to the first of the two questions with which this chapter began, the source of universal moral principles, it is often claimed that they have to do with the nature of things elucidated by rational reflection. I remember my first encounter with Aristotelian notions of matter and form, to me incomprehensible. I asked a colleague, "What's all this about matter and form?" "That's just the way things are," he replied. This assumption is not uncommon in relation to moral principles. I suspect that their real source is a craving for order and security in face of the disturbing flux of existence. Allegiance to principles generates the illusion that life is under our control. Someone once said to me, "I'm excited by what you say, but I can't go that far. I want some landmarks." Perhaps the intensity of the desire for moral landmarks actually brings them into being, or at least fosters the unexamined assumption that they are part of the timeless and universal nature of things.

The appeal to principles is implicitly away from a present of allegedly declining standards and selfish materialism to a time when principles held sway. But when was this? Whence comes this image of a human world ruled by principles? Certainly not from history: the more that is known about our past the less credible this picture becomes. In any case, why should it be supposed that principles have such ordering and controlling power? Does it not make sense to regard them as part of a particular culture's attempt to understand and perpetuate itself by claiming for itself a universal viewpoint? The thrust of the rallying cry about principles and standards is largely regressive. The unavoidable ambiguity in what is actually happening is short-circuited, not resolved, by this appeal.

To concentrate exclusively on the theme of rational moral agency leaves out of account most of what needs to be considered. Such concentration leaves us with nothing to say: if all we can say is that this act is evil we are only saying that we do not understand. One of the most chastening aspects of the Dunblane primary school massacre of 1996, as of many subsequent such events, was that the form taken by the public response to Thomas Hamilton's random shooting of many children made it hard to hold to the recognition that Hamilton too was a victim. The ready stigmatizing of his killing of those children, by church leaders and others, as distinctively evil, comes through as a refusal to look, to seek

2. Lean, dir., *Doctor Zhivago*.

to understand. What made Hamilton what he was? His mother, thinking to defend him or at least to make the best of her memories, said she had never known this man manifest anger towards anyone. What a scary predicament for a human being, to be so alienated from his own feelings! How he came to be thus remains mysterious, but we can be certain that there is a story to be told. The appeal to principle here is a distraction from the task of serious analysis of what is proceeding amongst us. Such analysis is often painful, but the reiterated appeal to universal moral principles merely avoids the necessary engagement.

24. FAMILY VALUES

LW

A STORY IN THE paper about a bishop in the Church of England whose wife has "run off" with someone else reminds me of what I hate about my church. Representatives are said to be "deeply saddened" by this "great tragedy" and to be praying for all concerned. The timing is particularly bad because the bishops have just issued a statement reiterating their disapproval of divorce and remarriage.

The church's stance is both less compassionate and less open-minded than that of wider society. Why the overblown rhetoric? How do they know that it is a "great tragedy"? It might involve liberation for all concerned, not to mention courage—we cannot know. The statement assumes too much and condemns too much. It separates off the speakers as righteous and innocent, and refuses to be attentive to ways in which the church may be implicated in the strains and stresses of a situation in which a bishop's wife no longer wishes to be a bishop's wife. If the language of tragedy is used in this context, what words are left with which to speak of what is worse?

Many churches have retreated into the role of sanctified guardian of family values as their wider influence has shrunk. This is ironic, given that so much of Christian tradition has often been suspicious of sex, marriage, and the family, if not downright hostile. Jesus commends celibacy (Matthew 19:10–12) and says that in the kingdom of heaven (that is now-and-still-to-come) "they neither marry nor are given in marriage (Mark 12:24–25). Paul suggests that "It is well for a man not to touch a woman" and that marriage is given as a remedy for sin (1 Corinthians 7:1–2). There is no evidence in the West of Christian marriage ceremonies in the first four centuries of Christian history and it was only in the eleventh century that a service in church started to become the norm.[1] Both the Western Roman Catholic tradition and the Eastern Orthodox tradition have always

1. Reynolds, "Marriage in the Western Church."

viewed celibacy as a higher state than marriage. So idealization of the nuclear family appears to be a Canute-like attempt to maintain some vestige of authority over people's lives, at least in the domestic sphere. The results for the divorced, the non-heterosexual, the unmarried, and Catholic couples wishing to use contraception, are hurtful and alienating.

This speaks of a failure of imagination, a failure to see possibilities of goodness and godliness in events, institutions, and people who do not conform to existing preconceptions of what is acceptable and "Christian." The institution of lifelong heterosexual marriage is endlessly commended. Those who find themselves outside it, or who reject it, must therefore be at fault, while those who stay within the boundaries of current church teaching are assumed to be virtuous. It is the mirror image of the failure to see the evil of sexual and domestic abuse: a failure to see both good and evil in unexpected places. Yet sin can flourish in even the most faithful and enduring marriages (remember Lord and Lady Macbeth) and amongst those at the very highest levels of the church.

In one of his most challenging comments, Bonhoeffer said that "the knowledge of good and evil seems to be the aim of all ethical reflection. The first task of Christian ethics is to invalidate this knowledge."[2] Paradoxically, the more scrupulously we obey the rules, the less our mind and heart are likely to be engaged. Every human society needs rules, principles, and laws in order to function, and every society arrives at different ones—but that is a sociological fact, not a theological one. Sometimes we cling to "moral standards" because we think we need them to protect us from ourselves and one another. But instead of allowing us to look openly at situations, moral law often tells us what to see. Concerns about social order are important, but to confuse social order with ethics is to deny the challenge of both.

Church leaders who sound warnings about modern societies drifting from the safe harbor of Christian values fear that we are plunging into swirling waters of chaos and immorality. But the preachers have cried wolf too often and predicted a slide into moral anarchy too many times. The reason people apologize for swearing in front of clergy is that they associate the church and its representatives with moralism and censorship. In some areas of life, including the way we treat children and deal with sexual abuse, there has been a notable advance on church teaching. I am often impressed by the way young people today discuss ethical issues and insist that whatever values one ascribes to, one must take responsibility

2. Bonhoeffer, *Ethics*, 3.

for them. I like the way they talk about doing the "right thing" or the "wrong thing" in relation to specific situations, rather than making universal judgments about good and evil.

The New Testament preserves traditions about Jesus that communicate something of his wildness and subversion. He is excoriating about official religion and its representatives and open to godliness in the most unexpected places: amongst sex workers and tax collectors, "sinners" and outcasts. When asked to make moral condemnations and rulings, he questions his interlocutors' motivations and issues crazy provocations instead. He often acts in defiance of convention and morality. It is not that he is an ethical lawgiver or a rebel against society's standards, for he does not operate within those categories at all.

25. A WORLD IN THE MAKING
NPH

I WAS BROUGHT UP a Roman Catholic with the idea that there was another world that, of course, included a notion of heaven; but this was distinctly ethereal compared to the idea that ruled me, that of a punishing God, unceasingly vigilant with a view to condemnation. At the same time the image of this world was of a place of suffering and temptation, a world in which, our catechism said, "our natural inclinations are prone to evil from our very childhood, and if not corrected by self-denial, they will certainly carry us to hell." In the "Hail, Holy Queen," recited nightly at the end of the rosary, we were pictured as "poor, banished children of Eve," "mourning and weeping in this vale of tears." So we were already judged, and suffering in consequence of that condemnatory judgment long ago.

The composite image of our predicament that resulted from all this now seems very strange, but in those days it had power. Life here was grim, but things were likely to be very much worse, and irreversibly so, in the next world unless one could somehow avoid giving in to the manifold occasions of grave sin by which we were surrounded. The task of avoidance seemed very much against the odds, especially in matters of sex, where "all wilful pleasure in the irregular motions of the flesh" was forbidden.

Later came exposure to talk of the beatific vision for which we were destined, but this could not drive out the miserable imagery of sin and hell that had become entrenched. In any case the suggestion of the beatific vision as the end of all our striving was unsatisfying. Aquinas situated this vision in the intellect, with an overflow into the other faculties, but the whole thing seemed cold and distant by comparison with known joys: the wonder of an unexpected sunset seen from high in the Cheviot hills, or of Slieve League against the early dawn sky seen from a fishing boat moving out from beneath it. Some mystics would argue that we have to withdraw from these and other more obviously sensual delights in order to be rapt in the vision of God. This is to invoke another and wholly spiritualized world that refuses full engagement with what is given.

If all true life flows from another and somehow higher world, is not most if not all of what proceeds here and now devalued? Whatever this "true life" is, it cannot be life in any sense we can find significant. A counter-argument might be that the reason the other world and its priorities has no purchase on my mind and heart is that I am still unconverted, or at best inadequately converted. But this is a strategy of avoidance, or a circular argument: it emerges from a closed system in which it is axiomatic that allegiance to the superiority of the other world is a mark of orthodoxy. On the contrary, I came to see that such allegiance is a distraction from and a dishonoring of the delight and tragedy of our part in the unfolding mystery, the becoming of all things. Conversion is a movement out of unreality into taking responsibility. For me this movement was prevented by preoccupation with another world.

Am I saying that the world as we know it satisfies all our desires and fulfills all our hopes? Not at all. What changed everything for me, ending my enslavement to the notion of the superiority of an unappealing other world, was the suggestion that this present world is a world in the making. It is hard to convey the excitement of encountering this claim for the first time, the liberation of emerging from a permanently overcast theological landscape into hope-filled daylight. Release from the assumption that there is another world, or that the existence of such a world is axiomatic for Christian belief, gave me hope. In retrospect the other world was always taking the edge off this one by inhibiting spontaneous responses. The image of a God who supplies standards and a frame of reference for moral condemnation from somewhere else is not conducive to wholehearted behavior.

It might be objected that my childhood version of Christianity was a gross distortion of the tradition. It was just my misfortune to be lumbered with such nonsense. But who is to adjudicate between the various versions of otherworldliness which have made headway in Christian history? Each variation on the theme should be given credit for responding to or interpreting something in the tradition, or at least in the corporate psyche of a significant grouping of those seriously engaged with the tradition. It is doctrinaire to dismiss any of them as merely and sheerly unorthodox without asking further questions, even though some of these turn out to be unanswerable. Thus, for instance, we cannot know what the Salve Regina was doing in the lives of those who originated it, but we must proceed on the assumption that it was doing something that mattered. The point for my purpose in this chapter is that we can get some sort of handle on what it was/is doing—or not doing—in our own lives.

A different way of dealing with this subject would be to look for grounds of agreement between my rejection of the idea of another world and the views of those who continue to uphold it. The suggestion that this is the best of all possible worlds in the making, or that this world is heaven in the making, gives center stage to ambitious possibilities. While always in danger of being translated into a deterministic optimism, it does not have to go that way. It does not mean that all is well, nor yet that everything necessarily will be well. Tragic outcomes are by no means denied, but those aspirations are given pride of place that would be deemed unattainable as long as the static perspective of two worlds obtains. It cannot be a matter of two worlds in any literal sense: this one here and the other one somewhere else. But it is possible that one function of the language of another world could be to draw attention to otherwise unsuspected and liberating possibilities in the present quite beyond the horizon of routine, anxious consciousness. From the point of view of the latter such possibilities might best be called impossibilities, certainly not attainable by any immediate conscious effort. But faith, we are told, can move mountains.

26. WHAT'S WRONG WITH PLAYING GOD?

LW

WHAT DOES IT MEAN to say that our world is a "creation," as Christians do? In a lifetime's experience of sitting in church, I never received a sniff of a suggestion that faith had anything to do with being creative, or that God is still actively creating. The days of Christian art and poetry seemed well and truly over. Divine creativity was relegated to the mists of Genesis or the once-for-all work of the cross. All that remained for us was to make sure that God's work was properly respected and revered. It was grateful obedience that was called for, not creative action.

When I was studying theology at university in the late 1980s, some scholarly big guns were busy defending the idea of creation as given and ordered. They were fighting against reproductive technologies and other innovations that, they said, threatened the natural order. This was not just a Catholic enterprise but a Protestant one, too. The Pope, Germain Grisez, and Oliver O'Donovan were in underlying agreement that humans should not "interfere" with what God has established. "Don't play God" was the watchword. The important work of creation and redemption was said to have been already carried out by God; all that humans seemed to do was mess it up. Whether it was the nuclear family or genetic diseases, the concern was that we should not "meddle." The "created order" calls for respect rather than improvement.

There is insight here. Our world far exceeds human powers of creation and control, whatever today's technological optimists in Silicon Valley might say. Wonderful and terrible things happen in spite of us, as we stand helplessly by. As a species, we have made disastrous interventions. The destruction of species and habitats, the warming of sea and atmosphere, the creation of dangerous substances that we cannot control—all are byproducts of what was naively called "progress." The need to stand back and see ourselves set in the larger landscapes of which we are a fleeting part has never seemed more important. But the idea that we have no role to play in creation does not follow.

In classical Chinese painting, humans appear as small figures within huge landscapes, part of an overall harmony. That harmony is neither static nor passive. Treating the world as a largely finished work strips us of an active role in a situation of constant change. If creation is over and done with, then we can only look back to a perfect blueprint of origins or forward to apocalyptic destruction and divine re-creation. Our role in the creative process is diminished, and with it much that makes us most human.

Although Christianity must take its share of the blame for promoting the idea of a law-bound universe, science took up the metaphor of "laws" of nature too. It brought laws within the grasp of a scientific rather than theological imagination, but the underlying image of law-like nature remained. The transition was from the idea of a creation that can be understood by participation in divine wisdom to a nature amenable to human reason and control. An underlying continuity remains. Though creationists may rail against evolutionary science and scientific atheists may fulminate against religion, they share an unacknowledged agreement that only certain ordained experts can decipher the laws of the universe and secure the future, whether by the book of science or that of Scripture.

But underlying ideas of nature and creation are changing, along with scientific self-understanding. The ecologist Emma Marris offers a profound critique of the idea of a pristine "nature." She recalls a moment of epiphany when she was working with colleagues in Hawaii to secure the future of native flora and fauna struggling to survive in the face of human cultivation and the introduction of "alien" species.[1] Their aim was to return some parts of the islands to a more "natural" state, a demanding task that involved the destruction of trees, vegetation, rabbits, foxes, cats, and many other living things. Marris began to have her doubts. They crystallized one day as she and the team drove up a mountain pass to overlook a breathtaking view of flowers cascading down a waterfall, framed by purple-leaved banana plants and ferns in vivid greens. At the sight of a sign by the highway saying "scenic byway" Marris's colleagues broke into hoots of derisory laughter: they detested the celebration of this "man-made" landscape. That was the moment she realized that they had all been trained not to see such

---

1. Marris, "Nature is Everywhere." See also Marris, *Rambunctious Garden.*

beauty. True, this ecosystem was not pristine and original, but what was? It had a beauty and integrity of its own. Why should the fact that human involvement has shaped it make it unnatural? It was the start of a journey towards a different understanding.

In her subsequent work, Marris offers an approach in which we do not disconnect ourselves from something outside us called the "environment" or distinguish "real" nature from the rest. She no longer drives her children to "nature reserves" but encourages them to root around for plants, bugs, and small creatures in the empty lots and abandoned corners of the American city where they live. On a disused stilt railway above street level they come across a little paradise: an ecosystem with forty different species of plants. Marris's recipe for landscape management today is to balance different strategies: preservation and rewilding, human cultivation, and space for new ecosystems to flourish and do their own thing. With the uncertainties of disease, climate change, and loss of species hanging over us, she believes that this mixed approach offers the best chance of creative adjustment.

The neat boundaries we have tried to erect between human and animal, culture and nature are breaking down. Scientific discovery is helping. The mapping of the human genome revealed that we share a huge percentage of DNA with the fruit fly and that we are closer than first cousins to the primates. Birdsong imitates car alarms and ring tones, and foxes and other clever species have adapted to exploit human environments. Dogs and other domestic animals co-evolved with us humans. Slowly, we are beginning to see ourselves as part of an ongoing stream of creative adaptations in which we play a role. A sense of wonder at what is beyond our control mixes with a sense of the importance of human creativity—for good and ill—in what some now speak of as the Anthropocene Era.

This post-Enlightenment picture encourages an understanding of human beings as both puny and powerful. Our species is capable of actions befitting both heaven and hell. We have tiny brains that cannot comprehend a fraction of what is "out there," yet we have made amazing discoveries and inventions. We are anxious yet supremely adaptable. We make a difference to history, while being daunted by the complex problems now facing us.

This more modest, interconnected way of looking at things calls for a renewal of the concept of creation, understood now not as an unchanging natural or God-given order but as mutually shaping processes. "Creation" with a small "c" may yet turn out to be a more useful and adaptable concept than "nature" or "environment." And the so-called argument from design will come to be seen as a weak rendering of a sense of wonder at creative process. As Annie Dillard puts it in her lyrical version of natural theology:

> I salt my breakfast eggs. All day long I feel created. I can see the blown dust on the skin on the back of my hand . . . There are some created sheep in the pasture below me . . . Created gulls pock the air, rip great curved seams in the settled air: I greet my created meal, amazed.[2]

The natural law approach I absorbed at university was full of strictures about "playing God," but did not pause to ask why we should be so careful not to imitate the deity. What kind of a God must this be? An omni-God who orders, controls, dominates, and disposes. It would be terrifying and tyrannical for any human being to assume such a role. But why worship such a being in the first place—"a god less lovable than a grasshead, who treats us less well than we treat our lawns."[3] The toleration of a morally intolerable God suggests a residual longing for someone in control: God as the ultimate protection, a mega Mafia boss. Part of us wants to believe that it will all come out right in the end, if we just do what we are told.

Creation has been too closely identified with nature, both by theologians and by scientists. The concept needs to be set on fire again. The opening chapters of Genesis do not have to be read merely as origin stories, as if creation happened once for all a long time ago. There are creation texts throughout the Bible.[4] Creative work is not done and dusted when the seven days of creation end. Some Christians talk as if there was a "fall," something like a bad car crash, after which the best that can be hoped for is restoration work by Jesus, the second Adam. In that way of thinking our only option is to say "thanks or no thanks" for the saving work that has been done. A different reading experiences divine forces continually active within a creation which, as Paul says, "groans and travails" as it repeatedly re-creates and resurrects itself.[5] The end is not foreordained. The promised kingdom, the perfect city, the peaceful garden, is shaped by forces, human and non-human, that act against the never-ending forces of destruction and decay, in a process whose outcome remains open.

2. Dillard, *Holy the Firm,* 25.

3. Dillard, *Holy the Firm,* 46.

4. See Westermann, *Creation.*

5. Romans 8:22.

Acknowledgments

The authors owe a debt of gratitude to many friends and colleagues with whom they have discussed ideas and drafts, sometimes at the Association for Teachers of Moral Theology and the Society for the Study of Christian Ethics.

Special thanks are due to Janet Fife for her expert copy-editing, trouble-shooting and permission-seeking; David and Karen Parker for indexing and winkling out the hardest-to-find errors; Iain Torrance for encouraging us, not least by finding supportive ways of asking 'and when is your book coming out?'.

Bibliography

Ahmari, Sohrab. *From Fire by Water: My Journey to the Catholic Faith.* San Francisco: Ignatius, 2019.

Annan, Noel. *Our Age: Portrait of a Generation.* London: Weidenfeld and Nicolson, 1990.

Auden, W. H. *The Age of Anxiety: A Baroque Eclogue.* Princeton, NJ: Princeton University Press, 2011.

Augustine, *The City of God.* Translated by Henry Bettenson. Harmondsworth: Penguin, 1972.

Babb, Luke. "Sacred Space." July 12, 2019. https://wildhunt.org/2019/07/column-sacred-space.html.

Baggini, Julian. "Blair's Philosophy." *The Guardian,* January 12, 2006. https://www.theguardian.com/society/2006/jan/12/publicservices.politics.

Barnes, Timothy. *Constantine and Eusebius.* Cambridge, MA: Harvard University Press, 2006.

Barth, Karl. *Church Dogmatics* II/1. Edinburgh: T. and T. Clark, 1960.

Becking, Bob, et al., eds. *Only One God? Monotheism in Ancient Israel and the Veneration of the Goddess Asherah.* Sheffield: Sheffield Academic, 2002.

Bernard, Stephen. *Paper Cuts: A Memoir.* London: Penguin, 2018.

Billingham, Richard. *Ray's A Laugh.* Zurich: Scalo, 2000.

Bonhoeffer, Dietrich. *Ethics.* London: SCM, 1963.

———. *Letters and Papers from Prison.* London: SCM, 2001.

Borsje, Jacqueline. "Monotheistic to a Certain Extent: The 'Good Neighbours' of God in Ireland." In *The Boundaries of Monotheism: Interdisciplinary Explorations into the Foundations of Western Monotheism*, edited by Anne-Marie Korte and Maaike de Haardt, 53–82. Leiden: Brill, 2009.

Brown, Peter. *The Body and Society.* New York: Columbia University Press, 1988.

Butt, Riazat. "Catholic church caught in new row over gay marriages." *The Guardian,* November 17, 2011. https://www.theguardian.com/world/2011/nov/17/catholic-church-row-gay-marriages.

Catholic Church. *The Penny Catechism.* https://www.olvrc.com/reference/catechism.html.

Church of England. "Oath of Allegiance." https://www.churchofengland.org/more/policy-and-thinking/canons-church-england/section-c.

———. "The Consecration of Bishops." https://www.churchofengland.org/prayer-and-worship/worship-texts-and-resources/book-common-prayer/ordaining-and-consecrating-1.

Colley, Linda. *Captives: Britain, Empire and the World 1600–1850.* London: Pimlico, 2002.

Collins, Peter. "An Analysis of Hospital Chapel Prayer Requests." In *A Sociology of Prayer*, edited by Giuseppe Giordan and Linda Woodhead, 191–212. Aldershot: Ashgate, 2015.

Congar, Yves. *I Believe in the Holy Spirit.* Vol. III. New York: Seabury, 1983.

Crossan, John Dominic. *Jesus: A Revolutionary Biography.* New York: Harper Collins, 2009.

Day, Abby. *The Religious Lives of Older Laywomen: The Last Active Anglican Generation.* Oxford: Oxford University Press, 2017.

Denton, William. *Is Spiritualism True?* Boston: William Denton, 1871.

Dillard, Annie. *Holy the Firm.* New York: Harper and Row, 1988.

Dreher, Rod. "What Must Survive a Corrupt Catholic Church." *New York Times*, August 15, 2018. https://www.nytimes.com/2018/08/15/opinion/catholic-church-sex-abuse-pennsylvania.

Dubisch, Jill. "Can There Be Religion Without Gender?" *In Contemporary Encounters in Gender and Religion,* edited by Lena Gemzöe, et al., 31–51. London: Palgrave MacMillan, 2016.

Duffy, Eamon. *Fires of Faith: Catholic England under Mary Tudor.* New Haven, CT: Yale University Press, 2009.

Dumitriu, Petru. *To the Unknown God.* London: William Collins, 1982.

Elliot, Marianne. *The Catholics of Ulster: A History.* London: Basic, 2002.

Emezi, Akwaeke. *Freshwater.* London: Faber and Faber, 2018.

Finaldi, Gabriele. *The Image of Christ.* London: National Gallery, 2000.

Fish, Stanley. *Is There a Text in This Class? The Authority of Interpretive Communities.* Cambridge, MA: Harvard University Press, 1990.

Fitzpatrick, P. J. *In Breaking of Bread.* Cambridge: Cambridge University Press, 2015.

Fox, Matthew. *Original Blessing: A Primer in Creation Spirituality.* Rev. ed. New York: Tarcher Putnam, 2000.

Fowl, Stephen. "Reconstructing and Deconstructing the Quest of the Historical Jesus." *Scottish Journal of Theology* 42, no 3 (August 1989) 319–33. https://www.cambridge.org/core/journals/scottish-journal-of-theology/article/abs/reconstructing-and-deconstructing-the-quest-of-the-historical-jesus/.

Fuchs, Josef. *Christian Morality: The Word Becomes Flesh.* Dublin: Gill and MacMillan, 1987.

Gibb, Moira. *An Abuse of Faith: The Independent Peter Ball Review.* Dame Moira Gibb, June 2017. https://www.churchofengland.org/media/3999908/report-of-the-peter-ball-review-210617.pdf.

Gilligan, Carol. *The Birth of Pleasure: A New Map of Love.* London: Chatto and Windus, 2012.

Goffin, Magdalen. *Watkin Path: An Approach to Belief.* Eastbourne: Sussex Academic, 2006.

Harvey, Nicholas Peter. *Death's Gift.* Grand Rapids: Eerdmans, 1985, 1995.

———. *The Morals of Jesus.* London: Darton, Longman & Todd, 1991.

Hauerwas, Stanley. *After Christendom? How the Church is to Behave If Freedom, Justice and a Christian Nation are Bad Ideas.* Nashville: Abingdon, 1991.

———. *The Peaceable Kingdom.* Notre Dame, IN: University of Notre Dame Press, 1983.

Heaney, Seamus. *The Cure at Troy: Sophocles' Philoctetes.* London: Faber and Faber, 2018.

———. "Out of This World." In *District and Circle.* London: Faber and Faber, 2006.

Hibbert, Christopher. *The Roots of Evil: A Social History of Crime and Punishment.* London: Greenwood, 1978.

Hill, Susan. *Jacob's Room Is Full of Books: A Year of Reading.* Kindle ed. London: Profile, 2017.

Howard, Elizabeth Jane. *Slipstream: A Memoir.* London: MacMillan, 2002.

Hume, David. *Dialogues Concerning Natural Religion.* New York: Hafner, 1948.

Inquiry into Chichester Diocese. Transcript. https://www.iicsa.org.uk/key-documents/ 4385/view/8-march-2018-anglican-public-hearing-transcript.pdf.

Jenkins, Philip. *Pedophiles and Priests: Anatomy of a Contemporary Crisis.* Oxford: Oxford University Press, 2001.

———. "The Road from Damascus." Intercollegiate Studies Institute, August 19, 2019. https://isi.org/modern-age/the-road-from-damascus.

John Paul II. *Pastoral Visit of John Paul II to Ukraine 2001.* Holy Mass—Chayka Airport, Kyiv. June 24, 2001. https:www.vatican.va/content/john-paul-ii/en/travels/2001.

Jones, David. *The Anathemata: Fragments of an Attempted Writing.* London: Faber and Faber, 2010.

Julian of Norwich. *A Revelation of Love.* Edited by Marion Glascoe. Exeter: University of Exeter Press, 1976.

Jungel, Eberhard. *Karl Barth: A Theological Legacy.* Translated by Garrett E. Paul. Philadelphia: Westminster, 1986.

Kaiser, Robert Blair. "Review of John R. Quinn 'The Reform of the Papacy: The Costly Call to Christian Unity.'" Wijngaards Institute for Catholic Research, Women Can Be Priests. https://womenpriests.org/womens-ministry/kaiser-the-reform-of-the-papacy-the-costly-call-to-christian-unity/.

Kavanagh, P. J. *The Perfect Stranger.* London: Quartet, 1973.

Keenan, Marie. *Child Sexual Abuse and the Catholic Church: Gender, Power and Organisational Culture.* New York: Oxford University Press, 2011.

Kelly, Kevin T. *Divorce and Second Marriage.* London: Bloomsbury/Geoffrey Chapman, 1996.

Kierkegaard, Søren. *Fear and Trembling.* Harmondsworth: Penguin, 1985.

Kingsford, Anna. *Clothed with the Sun.* London: John M. Watkins, 1889.

Lean, David, dir. *Doctor Zhivago.* London: MGM-Britain, 1965.

Lehmann, Rosamund. *The Swan in the Evening: Fragments of an Inner Life.* Rev. ed. London: Virago, 1982.

Lewis, C. S. *The Four Loves.* London: Geoffrey Bles, 1960.

Longley, Clifford. "Mozart was not just a musical genius." *The Tablet,* February 4, 2006.

MacIntyre, Alasdair. *After Virtue: A Study in Moral Theory.* London: Duckworth, 1981.

MacMullen, Ramsay. *Christianizing the Roman Empire (A.D. 100-400).* New Haven, CT: Yale University Press, 1984.

Maguire, Kevin. "Faith." In *The Experience of Prayer,* by Sebastian Moore and Kevin Maguire, 53. London: Darton, Longman and Todd, 1969.

Mahoney, John. *The Making of Moral Theology: A Study of the Roman Catholic Tradition.* Oxford: Clarendon, 1999.

Mantel, Hilary. *Fludd.* New York: Viking, 1989.

Marris, Emma. "Nature is Everywhere—We Just Need to Learn to See It." TEDSummit, June 2016. https://www.ted.com/talks/emma_marris_nature_is_everywhere_we_ just_need_to_learn_to_see_it?language=en.

————. *Rambunctious Garden: Saving Nature in a Post-Wild World.* London: Bloombury, 2013.

McDonagh, Enda. *Gift and Call.* Dublin: Gill, 1975.

Moore, Sebastian. *The Contagion of Jesus: Doing Theology as if it Mattered.* London: Darton, Longman and Todd, 2007.

————. *Let This Mind be in You: Quest for Identity Through Oedipus to Christ.* London: Darton, Longman and Todd, 1985.

Nagasawa, Yujin. *Maximal God: A New Defence of Perfect Being Theism.* Oxford: Oxford University Press, 2017.

Nygren, Anders. *Agape and Eros.* Translated by Philip S. Watson. London: Harper Torch, 1953.

O'Donovan, Oliver. *Resurrection and Moral Order.* Leicester: InterVarsity, 1986.

O'Loughlin, Thomas. "Christ and the Scriptures: The Chasm between Modern and Pre-modern Exegesis." *The Month* (December 1998) 475–85.

Orr, Deborah. *Motherwell.* London: Weidenfeld and Nicolson, 2020.

O'Toole, James, ed. *Habits of Devotion: Catholic Religious Practice in Twentieth Century America.* Ithaca, NY: Cornell University Press, 2005.

Parker, David. *The Living Text of the Gospels.* Cambridge: Cambridge University Press, 2008.

————. "Textual Criticism and Theology." In *Manuscripts, Texts, Theology. Collected Papers 1977-2007,* 323–26. Berlin and New York: De Gruyter, 2009.

————. *Textual Scholarship and the Making of the New Testament.* Oxford: Oxford University Press, 2014.

Pearse, Pádraig. *The Singer.* https://celt.ucc.ie//published/E950004-001/index.html.

Phillips, Adam. *On Balance.* London: Hamish Hamilton, 2010.

————. *Winnicott.* London: Penguin, 2007.

Raven, Charles. *Teilhard de Chardin: Scientist and Seer.* New York and London: Harper & Row, 1962.

Rawnsley, Andrew. "The Scottish Nationalists Take the Sly Road to Independence." *The Guardian,* October 18, 2015. https://www.theguardian.com/commentisfree/2015/oct/18/snp-conference-referendum-issue.

Reynolds, P. L. "Marriage in the Western Church: the Christianization of Marriage During the Patristic and Early Medieval Times." *Journal of Ecclesiastical History* 47 (1996) 338–40.

Robinson, Marilynne. *When I Was a Child I Read Books.* London: Virago, 2013.

Saiving-Goldstein, Valerie. "The Human Situation: A Feminine View." *Journal of Religion* 40, no. 2 (April 1960) 100–112.

Schlieter, Jens. *What Is It Like to Be Dead? Near-Death Experiences, Christianity, and the Occult.* Oxford: Oxford University Press, 2018.

Schüssler Fiorenza, Elisabeth. *Jesus: Miriam's Child, Sophia's Prophet: Critical Issues in Feminist Christology.* London: Continuum, 1994.

Schweitzer, Albert. *The Quest of the Historical Jesus.* 3rd ed. London: Adam and Charles Black, 1973.

Scott, Matthew. "'Beating Posh Boys for Jesus': John Smyth and his Fanatical Evangelicalism." http://barristerblogger.com/2017/02/09/beating-posh-boys-jesus-john-smyth-fanatical-evangelicalism/.

Sharlet, Jeff. *The Family: Secret Fundamentalism at the Heart of American Power.* New York: Harper, 2008.

Sherwood, Harriet. "C of E Bishop: I was Given 'Excruciating Beating by John Smyth.'" *The Guardian,* February 6, 2016. https://www.theguardian.com/uk-news/2017/feb/06/c-of-e-bishop-guildford-andrew-watson-excruciating-beating-john-smyth.

———. "Top Catholic School Stripped of Pupil Welfare Responsibilities." *The Guardian,* April 4, 2018. https://www.theguardian.com/education/2018/apr/04/topcatholic-school-stripped-of-pupil-welfare-responsibilities.

Siedentop, Larry. *Inventing the Individual: The Origins of Modern Liberalism.* Cambridge, MA: Belknap, 2014.

Smith, Stevie. "Oh Christianity, Christianity." In *Collected Poems and Drawings of Stevie Smith.* London: Faber and Faber, 2015.

Smith, Wilfred Cantwell. *The Meaning and End of Religion: A New Approach to the Religious Traditions of Mankind.* New York: New American Library, 1964.

Strhan, Anna. *Aliens and Strangers: The Struggle for Coherence in the Everyday Lives of Evangelicals.* Oxford: Oxford University Press, 2015.

Stringer, Martin. *Contemporary Western Ethnography and the Definition of Religion.* London: Continuum, 2011.

Stuart, Elizabeth. *Just Good Friends.* Bristol: Mowbray, 1995.

Trible, Phyllis. *Texts of Terror: Literary-Feminist Readings of Biblical Narratives.* Minneapolis: Fortress, 1984.

Taylor, Charles. *A Secular Age.* Cambridge, MA: Belknap Press of Havard University Press, 2007.

van der Toorn, Karel, et al., eds. *Dictionary of Deities and Demons in the Bible.* 2nd ed. Leiden: Brill-Eerdmans, 1998.

Vermes, Géza. *Jesus the Jew.* London: Collins, 1973.

Voas, David, and Mark Chaves. "Is the United States a Counterexample to the Secularization Thesis?" *American Journal of Sociology* 121, no. 5 (March 2016) 1517–56.

Wallace, Mark I. *When God Was a Bird: Christianity, Animism and the Re-enchantment of the World.* New York: Fordham University Press, 2018.

Walter, Tony. "Angels not Souls: Popular Religion in the Online Mourning for British Celebrity Jade Goody." *Religion* 41, no. 1 (2011) 29–51.

Waugh, Evelyn. *Brideshead Revisited.* London: Penguin Classics, 2011.

Westermann, Claus. *Creation.* London: SPCK, 1974.

Winnicott, D. W. "Communicating and Not Communicating." In *The Maturational Processes and the Facilitating Environment: Studies in the Theory of Emotional Development,* 179–92. London: Hogarth, 1965.

Woodhead, Linda. "Love and Justice." *Studies in Christian Ethics* 5, no. 1 (1992) 44–61.

———. "Rape Followed by Bureaucracy—Matthew's Story." In *Letters to a Broken Church,* edited by Janet Fife and Gilo, 101–5. London: Ekklesia, 2019.

Index of Names and Subjects

Scripture Index

Printed in Great Britain
by Amazon

86466154R00093